DATE DUE

OCT 1	APR 04		
OCT 30	DEC 18		
NOV 18	OCT 03		
MAY 18	MAY 4		
SEP 12	MAY 21		
NOV 7	MAY 11		
APR 22			
MAR 24			
APR 17			
JAN 0			

THE MYSTERIES OF REINCARNATION

THE MYSTERIES OF REINCARNATION

Daniel Cohen

Illustrated with photographs and reproductions

DODD, MEAD & COMPANY
New York

Illustration Credits

The illustrations in this book are used by permission and through the courtesy of the following: Library of Congress, 6, 31, 64; New York Public Library Picture Collection, 2, 4, 29, 52, 58, 66, 69, 79; The Society for Psychical Research, 34; United Press International Photo, 9, 104, 123; University of Virginia, Office of Public Information, 144. The handwriting examples on pages 84, 88, 90, 91, 93, 94, and 97 are from the book, *From India to the Planet Mars*, by Theodore Flournoy, University Books.

Library of Congress Cataloging in Publication Data

Cohen, Daniel.
The mysteries of reincarnation.

Bibliography: p.
Includes index.
1. Reincarnation. I. Title.
BL515.C58 129'.4 74-25517
ISBN 0-396-07077-9

Printed in the United States of America

To Peter and Rhita

Contents

THE MYSTERIES OF REINCARNATION

1

Have You Lived Before?

Many people have said that they know reincarnation is a fact because they can remember their own previous existences. They have described lives as queens of France, Roman soldiers, ancient Egyptian priests, even inhabitants of the lost continent of Atlantis and the planet Mars. All of these accounts and many more are going to be discussed in the pages that follow. But I would like to start out with a short, simple, and undramatic account. I begin with it because it happened to me, and possibly something similar has once happened to you—or will happen.

When I was about fourteen years old I dreamed that I was a member of the crew of an ancient Greek ship. The ship was an open one propelled by a single bank of oarsmen. It was the sort of ship one might imagine Ulysses and his men had used when returning from Troy.

I remember sitting on a hard wooden bench clutching an oar, and looking over at my fellow crewmen also seated at their oars. We were all dark-skinned or deeply tanned from our long exposure to the hot Aegean sun. Years of strenuous physical labor had made us lean and muscular.

At the time, in my waking life, I had a skin the color of parchment because I sunburned easily and avoided exposure to the sun at all costs. I was also overweight with no identifiable muscles showing. What had a bookish teen-ager from Chicago to do with this rugged sea-going adventurer? Yet in my dream I *was* that man.

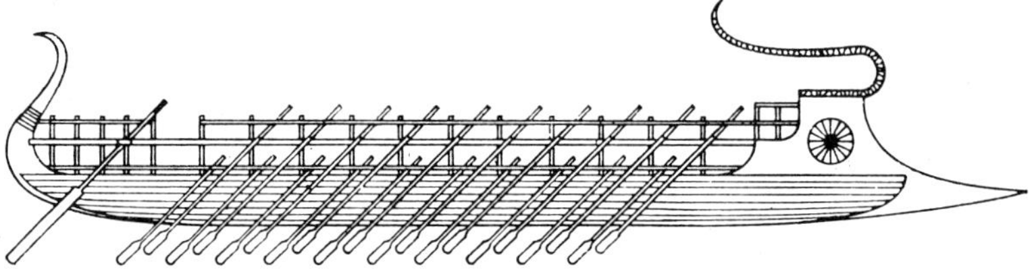

The ship in my dream was an open one propelled by a single bank of oarsmen.

Our ship was cruising near shore and I could see a city in the distance, though its outlines were somewhat hazy. I recall that it reminded me of drawings I had seen of Renaissance Florence, which surely would have been out of place in Homeric Greece, but that is how I remember my dream. Don't forget, I couldn't see the city too clearly.

Nothing happened in my dream, or at least nothing that I remembered. We just seemed to be floating there, and then I woke up. Yet the dream left an extraordinary impression on me. All the next day I had to keep reminding myself that it was just a dream, not something that had really happened. For weeks afterward I could find myself slipping into the feeling that not long ago I had been a Greek sailor. Even today, nearly a quarter of a century later, I can still recall the scene as clearly and freshly as if I had dreamed it last night.

One might argue that this sort of a dream, in which I had been transformed from my humdrum, unheroic self into some sort of ancient swashbuckler is the most obvious form of wish fulfillment dream. Rationally, I feel compelled to agree that it was nothing more than that. But a mere description of the dream does not adequately convey the feeling that it gave me.

I am not the sort of person who remembers his dreams very well. Before I learned that science had discovered that everyone dreams several times every night, and the only difference is that some people remember their dreams well while others do not, I was under the impression that I hardly dreamed at all. In my entire life I have not had more than a handful of really vivid dreams. Aside from this one, most of the few vivid dreams I did have concerned immediate things—anxieties, hopes, fears, and desires related directly to my day-to-day life. I am, it appears, a rather unimaginative dreamer.

Though I have always been interested in history, and was certainly aware of the ancient Greeks, I had not read anything about them immediately prior to my dream. In fact, I have never been particularly drawn to that period of history. If I were to pick a time and place into which to project my wish fulfillment fantasies it would not be Homeric Greece.

Why then, did this exotic but uneventful and thoroughly uncharacteristic dream stick with me? I have often entertained the idea that it was more than a dream, that it was a memory of a past life.

Perhaps you have had that same feeling at some time or another, though it may not have been triggered by a dream. You may have felt out of place in the twentieth century, and that you were really "meant for" some other time. You may possess a strong affinity for a particular time in history.

The dream of having been a sailor in ancient Greece left an extraordinary impression on me.

Possibly you went to a place that you had never been before and then quite suddenly felt or "knew" that you had been there before. This experience, known by the French term *déjà vu,* is extremely common. A recent survey taken by the University of Chicago's National Opinion Research Center indicated that 61 per cent of a representative sample of the United States population has at one time or another experienced such a feeling. One theory has been that the feeling of *déjà vu* comes when you visit a place that you remember from a former life.

Have you ever met someone for the first time, and felt that you had known this person all of your life? This may have made you suspect that you really had known the person before, but not in this life.

There are those who have more than occasional feelings too. General George Patton, the crusty and eccentric World War II hero, was absolutely convinced that he had been a warrior and soldier in past ages. From childhood he was quite sure that he was destined to be a military leader in this life as well.

General Patton said that he could remember fighting with the Greeks on the plains of Troy. In other incarnations he had served in Caesar's legions, he had battled the Huns, ridden with the Crusaders to the Holy Land, and fought with the Highland Scots in defense of the House of Stuart.

Though a lot of people would undoubtedly regard such a belief as more than a little crazy, Patton never made any secret of it. When his nephew asked him point-blank if he really believed in reincarnation, Patton answered, "I don't know about other people; but for myself there has never been any question. I just don't think it, I damn well know there are places I've been before, and not in this life."

The general then went on to recount an incident that had taken place at the time he assumed his first command. It was at the French town of Langres, where there were some impressive ancient Roman ruins.

A French liaison officer offered to show Patton around the ruins. He declined, saying, "You don't have to. I know this place. I know it well." Though he had never been there before, as George Patton anyway, he was then able to direct his driver around the site and point out the old Roman amphitheater, the drill ground, the forum, and the temples of Mars and Apollo.

As evidence that General George Patton had indeed visited the site with Caesar's legions in a previous existence, this incident does not stand up very well. Roman military garrisons were built according to a rigid plan, one that certainly would have been very familiar to as keen a student of military history as George Patton. Therefore, it is not unlikely that Patton, un-

Lt. Gen. George S. Patton, Jr. in 1943

consciously recalling the plan of Roman garrisons, was able to find his way about this site with what appeared to be uncanny accuracy.

But such an explanation would not have had any effect upon General Patton. He was not looking for evidence of reincarnation. He did not need any because he knew that he had lived before. His complete conviction of his past and future lives as a warrior is expressed quite forcefully in a poem called "Through a Glass Darkly," which he wrote in 1944.

> So as through a glass and darkly
> The age-long strife I see
> Where I fought in many guises
> Many names—but always me.
>
> . . . . .
>
> So forever in the future,
> Shall I battle as of yore,
> Dying to be born a fighter
> But to die again once more.

General Patton's total and outspoken acceptance of reincarnation is a bit unusual for an American. In the Western world reincarnation is not really an accepted or acceptable belief. Though many people actually do believe in reincarnation, it is not part of prevailing religious beliefs. Indeed Christianity has usually been quite hostile to the idea of reincarnation.

In lands like Tibet (before it was taken over by the materialistically-minded Communists) reincarnation was not only believed in, it was acted upon.

The Dalai Lama was considered the supreme spiritual leader of the Tibetans. When the Dalai Lama died, it was assumed that his soul would return again in another body to guide his people.

So immediately upon the death of a reigning Dalai Lama, a search was instituted among Tibetan children born at approximately the time the Dalai Lama died, for it was assumed that the departed lama's soul would almost immediately reincarnate in another body.

The searchers first looked for particular physical signs, such as markings like the stripes of a tiger on the child's legs. The search usually took years, and in the end there were several candidates for the honor. It was believed that the true incarnation would be able to pick out objects used by the Dalai Lama in his past life, from an assortment of similar objects laid before him.

This process of selection, however, was rarely pure or honest. It was generally believed that politics rather than any signs or tests determined which of the candidates was to be chosen the new spiritual leader. In addition, an unnaturally large number of Dalai Lamas died mysteriously while still very young. This led to the charge that the subordinate lamas, who wielded the real power while the Dalai Lama was still a child, were reluctant to give it up when he reached adulthood, so they killed him in order to be able to continue to exercise their power under a new child lama.

We in the West do not choose our religious leaders on the basis of their previous incarnations. As one regular churchgoer told me, we are not even "supposed" to believe in it. But a lot of people feel there is "something to" this reincarnation business anyway.

There is a great deal more to the subject of reincarnation than the occasional feelings of *déjà vu,* strange dreams, unexplainable affinities, or even more powerful emotions like those of

The current Dalai Lama as a child. The Dalai Lama is chosen as a child and is believed to be the reincarnation of the previous Dalai Lama.

General Patton. The subject is such an enormous one that in this book we are going to have to limit our exploration, and limit it sharply.

First, let us decide what reincarnation is not—it is not coming back to earth as a dog, or pig, or fly. The incarnation or rebirth of souls in other than human forms is often called transmigration. We will discuss transmigration briefly a little later on, but we must keep the distinction clearly in mind.

In this book we are going to concentrate primarily on reincarnation in the West, that is, in Europe and America, or on reincarnation cases that have been studied by Western investigators. This may seem a biased and narrow decision, particularly since reincarnation is traditionally associated with Eastern countries like India and Tibet, and some of the very best reincarnation case histories come out of these lands.

The reasons for a limited view are simple enough. The author of this book, as well as the vast majority of its readers come out of a Western cultural background. In the East a belief in reincarnation grows out of a religion and philosophy that goes back thousands of years. Without adequately understanding the religious and philosophical background upon which the Eastern beliefs are based, we run the risk of seriously misunderstanding the cases. Besides, there is plenty of material from the West to engage our attention.

We are also going to try to concentrate on fairly modern cases, for the very obvious reason that we have more information on modern cases than we do about ones that occurred a long time ago. As we shall see, in case after case, belief in reincarnation is by no means something out of the distant past or from some exotic land. There is even an effort at a scientific investigation of the subject.

The mere use of the words "scientific investigation" in connection with reincarnation, however, compels a few words of caution. There have been innumerable books and articles on reincarnation, which claim to present all manner of scientific "proof" of the reality of the phenomenon. But no reasonable person could look at the accumulated evidence mustered in support of reincarnation and say that the case has been proved in any sense of the term. The very best that can be said for the scientific evidence gathered so far is that it is "suggestive." Reincarnation may be put forth as one of several alternative explanations for the material, not as the only explanation.

While we are going to examine the best of the available evidence, it is important to recognize that the widespread current interest in reincarnation is not based so much on evidence as it is on the feeling that reincarnation is somehow "right" and that it "makes sense."

Since ancient times philosophers have clung to the idea that there is a perfection about nature, that nothing created is ever destroyed or wasted. Ice may be melted and turn to water, and then heated and made into steam, condensed back into water, then refrozen into ice. The form changes but the essential substance remains the same. If this could be done for all known substances in nature it seemed absurd to believe that a creation as noble and unique as the human soul could simply disappear after bodily death or even be taken permanently out of circulation by being placed in heaven or hell. Many find it far more logical to assume that the soul is in some way recycled through a series of bodies.

Reincarnation also appears to many to make excellent moral and ethical sense as well. Brad Steiger, a popular and prolific writer on occult subjects, has written, "Have you ever wondered why some people are born into wealthy families and have every comfort that life can offer, while others are born into dire poverty, with the proverbial "three strikes" against them? Why some have every advantage that money and social prestige can bestow, while others stumble along with little gain in life? Why some people live to extremely old age, while in another case a child is born, only to die within a few weeks or years, having accomplished nothing so far as one can tell?"

Reincarnation, many believe, can supply a hopeful answer to all of those painful questions.

Finally, and very persuasively, the idea is exciting. As I mentioned, Homeric Greece was not my favorite time in history, but I still find the thought that I was there, and at some future time will be somewhere else in another form, extremely attractive.

So we are going to look at the subject of reincarnation from two angles—the evidence such as it is, and the beliefs and feelings about it. We cannot prove (or disprove, for that matter) the theory of reincarnation. But by examining it, we can learn a good deal about how people in the past and present have approached and tried to solve such basic human problems as finding a meaning and purpose to life.

One of the primary reasons why interest in reincarnation appears to be higher today than it has been for some years is that so many of our traditional beliefs and values have been badly shaken. Cut adrift in a universe that looks increasingly chaotic, many have begun to take a new look at reincarnation in the hope that it will provide some answers, some security in life. Even if the phenomena itself does not exist, the belief in it most certainly does, and is worthy of our serious attention.

2

Reincarnation in the West

When the word "reincarnation" is mentioned, most of us would probably think first of India or some other "Eastern" or "Oriental" land. Reincarnation is a prominent feature of the Hindu religion, and it is also important in Buddhist philosophies. But it is not exclusively an Eastern belief.

The concept of the rebirth of the soul in many different bodies is an extremely ancient one. Some modern reincarnationists claim that a belief in successive rebirths formed the basis of mankind's original religion, though the claim is unprovable.

Ancient Greece is popularly regarded as the birthplace of Western civilization. Reincarnation was a popular doctrine there, particularly among those who claimed to be followers of the legendary singer Orpheus. There was a whole conglomeration of cults and sects that have been called Orphic. The origins of the Orphic beliefs are obscure, and there were tremendous variations. Many of the cults appeared to hold that the soul was immortal, but from time to time it became trapped and imprisoned in a body. Death freed the soul from its fleshly bonds, but the soul was again quickly reimprisoned in another body, and so on through eternity. To these Greeks death was freedom and rebirth was not something that one should look forward to.

The doctrine of reincarnation was a powerful influence among the followers of Pythagoras. Most people have heard of Pythagoras the mathematician, and were at one time or another required to memorize the Pythagorean theorem: "The square of the length of the hypotenuse of a right triangle is equal to the sum of the squares of the lengths of the other two sides."

But Pythagoras was not primarily a mathematician or, in fact, a mathematician in any modern sense at all. He was the leader of a small but extremely influential religious movement. A universe made up of mathematical unities was part of the religious doctrines of Pythagoras and his followers. While pursuing their vision of the unity of the universe, they made many important mathematical discoveries, but to the Pythagoreans such discoveries had a religious and mystical, rather than purely mathematical, importance.

We don't know a great deal about Pythagoras himself. Tradition holds that he was born on the Greek island of Samos sometime during the sixth century B.C. He is said to have traveled widely, particularly in Egypt, absorbing all sorts of ancient wisdom. In the year 529 B.C., the only solid date we have for Pythagoras' life, he went to Crotona, a Greek colony in southern Italy. There he gathered about him a group of disciples and formed the Pythagorean Brotherhood, though apparently women were also admitted.

Pythagoras worked hard at cloaking himself with an aura of awe and mystery. It was said that new disciples were not allowed to see him at all, but that he spoke to them only through a curtain. Even his most trusted associates were allowed to gaze upon him only at night.

A later writer described Pythagoras thus: "He appeared in a garment of the purest white, with a flowing beard and a garland upon his head. He is said to have been of the finest symmetrical form with majestic carriage and a grave and awful countenance. He suffered his followers to believe that he was one of the gods, the Hyperborean Apollo, and is said to have told [one of his disciples] that he had assumed human form that he might better invite men to an easiness of approach and confidence in him." There were numerous accounts of the miracles he performed. He was said to be able to become invisible at will, to walk upon water, and to make objects appear and disappear.

What all of this mumbo-jumbo was supposed to mean, or if indeed anyone really believed such things ever happened, we really don't know. Pythagoras never wrote anything, and everything that we know about his life is based on second and third-hand sources, often written down long after the Pythagorean Brotherhood itself had dissolved. Besides, tradition credits practically every ancient sage with the same sort of magical feats.

While the sources are quite consistent in claiming that the Pythagoreans were believers in reincarnation, we cannot be sure whether this belief also extended to the idea of transmigration, that is, the incarnation of souls in bodies other than human.

It has often been said that the Pythagorean Brotherhood preached the equality of slaves and of women, and kindness to animals, because they could never be sure in what form a soul might appear.

The belief that Pythagoras did teach transmigration was an unusually popular one. Nearly two thousand years after the death of Pythagoras, Shakespeare wrote in his play, *Twelfth Night*:

What is the opinion of Pythagoras concerning wild-fowl?
That the soul of our grandam might haply inhabit a bird.
What thinkest thou of his opinion?
I think nobly of the soul, and in no way approve of his opinion.

Shakespeare made a number of other references to this supposed teaching of Pythagoras in other plays, indicating that the subject was of considerable interest to sixteenth-century Englishmen.

Yet despite this widespread opinion, there is a good deal of contradictory evidence. A later Pythagorean named Hierocles wrote:

"He who believes that the soul transmigrates, after death, into the body of a beast or a plant is grossly mistaken; he is ignorant of the fact that the essential form of the soul cannot change, that it is and it remains human, and only metaphorically speaking does virtue make it a god and vice an animal."

But on reincarnation itself, that is, the rebirth of the soul in different human forms, the evidence is quite clear. An early compiler of the life of Pythagoras wrote:

"[Pythagoras] was accustomed to speak of himself in this manner that he had formerly been Aethalides . . . At a subsequent period, he was reborn as Euphorbus, and was wounded by Menelaus at the siege of Troy, and so died. In that life he used to say that he had formerly been Aethalides, and that he had received as a gift from Mercury (the god of wisdom) the memory of his soul's transmigration . . . also the gift of recollecting what his own soul and the souls of others had experienced between death and rebirth."

Obviously some sort of an idea of rebirth enjoyed considerable popularity among the ancient Greeks. Plato, the most influential of all Greek philosophers, discussed the subject extensively. In his most celebrated work, *The Republic,* Plato tells a story of a group of souls getting ready to choose the destiny of their next lives. In this tale the great hero Odysseus is the last to choose. "When he came up to choose, the memory of his former sufferings had so abated his ambition that he went about a long time looking for a quiet retired life, which with great trouble he discovered lying about, and thrown contemptuously aside by the others. As soon as he saw it, he chose it gladly, and said that he would have done the same if he had even drawn the first lot . . ."

The souls in Plato's story, having chosen their new lives, travel to the Plain of Forgetfulness and drink from the River of Indifference. After they have forgotten everything about their past lives, "there was a clap of thunder and an earthquake; and in a moment the souls were carried up to their birth, this way and that, like shooting stars."

Plato had not meant this particular tale to be taken literally. It was a story concocted to make some philosophical and moral points, but the mere fact that he set it within a framework of reincarnation indicates that the idea was well known to the Greeks.

One influential stream of Greek philosophic thought held that nothing was ever truly created or disappeared, but that everything changed form. Reincarnation squares neatly with such a concept.

Half the intellectual heritage of Europe comes from the Greeks and the Romans. The other half comes from the Jews and the Christians. In this half, evidence for a belief in reincarnation is much harder to find, though many modern reincarnationists have worked hard at finding some, so that they can support reincarnation with traditional religious beliefs.

Perhaps the closest one can come to a statement of reincarnationist beliefs in the Old Testament are a few lines from Eccles. 1:9-11. "The thing that hath been, it is that which shall be . . . and there is no new thing under the sun. Is there any thing whereof it may be said, See, this is new? It hath been already of old time, which was before us. There is no remembrance of former things."

One must strain a good deal in order to twist this rather general statement about the permanence of all things into a proof that the ancient Hebrews believed in reincarnation.

But the Old Testament represents only one current of thought in the ancient Jewish world, the one that ultimately triumphed, to be sure, but not the only one. There were many sects, philosophies, denominations, or whatever in the ancient Jewish world. Often the beliefs of the unorthodox were not reflected, or reflected only indirectly, in the Old Testament. We get only isolated glimpses of the numerous Jewish groups which subsequently disappeared from history.

Perhaps the best known of these early unorthodox movements were the Essenes. The Essenes were a rigidly ascetic communal group that existed in the Holy Land shortly before the time of Christ. The famous Dead Sea Scrolls discovered in the 1950s were attributed, wrongly it now appears, to the Essenes.

Most of what we know of this group comes from the writings of Flavius Josephus, a Jewish general who went over to the Romans, became a friend of the emperor, and lived to write a massive history of the Jewish people. Josephus is not widely liked today, because he is regarded as a traitor to his people, which in a sense he was. But nonetheless, he was a first-rate historian, whose books contain a wealth of information not otherwise available.

According to Josephus, the Essenes scorned all pleasures of life and were above pain. "They smiled in their very pains and laughed to scorn those who inflicted torments upon them, and resigned up their souls with great alacrity, as they expected to receive them again."

Josephus said that the Essenes viewed the body as corruptible, but the soul as immortal . . . "and that they [souls] come out of the most subtile air, and are united to their bodies as to prisons, into which they are drawn by a certain natural enticement; but that when they are set free from the bondage of flesh they then, as released from a long bondage, rejoice and mount upward . . ." Theirs was not a cheerful view of life.

The concept of reincarnation continued to play a part, though a minor one, in the speculations of Jewish religious thinkers for centuries. It surfaced once again in the Kabala, a collection of Jewish magical and mystical lore compiled primarily during the Middle Ages. The books of the Kabala are exceedingly, almost unbelievably, obscure. It has been said that no one who has ever immersed himself deeply in Kabalistic lore has ever emerged entirely sane. In any case, the Kabala has, at most, been a side branch of Jewish thought, more revered than studied.

Though most Kabalistic writing is open to a variety of interpretations, the idea of reincarnation emerges with reasonable clarity. Souls were to perfect themselves during various incarnations, until, in the words of the Kabalistic classic, *The Zohar*, "they have acquired the condition which fits them for reunion with God."

During the eighteenth and nineteenth centuries the Kabala attracted the attention of some Christians who were interested in the occult and magic. They made their own interpretations of the Jewish mystical writings, and the reincarnationist ideas they contained. These Christian Kabalists deeply influenced European occult thought. But we are running ahead of the story, and we will return to the occultists in a little while.

Some believers in reincarnation have asserted that the doctrine was supported, or at least implied, in the teachings of Jesus and his disciples. But the Biblical support for such an argument is exceedingly thin. One of the favorite New Testament citations of modern reincarnationists is in the book of John, where Jesus is brought into the presence of a man who had been born blind. The disciples wondered why this man was punished, since blindness was generally viewed as a punishment from God for some sin. They asked Jesus, "Which did sin, this man or his parents?" To Joseph Head and S. L. Cranston, two modern believers in reincarnation who have compiled the best anthology available on the subject, this question has great significance.

"The disciples must have had the idea of reincarnation in mind, for obviously if the man had been born blind, his sin could not have been committed in this life. If the doctrine was wrong and pernicious, then, it would seem, this was the time for Jesus to deny the whole theory. Yet he did not do so, although in this case he said the blindness was for other reasons."

What Jesus actually did reply was, "Neither hath this man sinned, nor his parents: but that the works of God should be manifest in him." Jesus then healed the man's blindness, much to the astonishment of his neighbors. So it seems that the man had not been born blind as a punishment for sins of a previous life, but had been put on earth blind specifically so that he could be healed by Jesus, in order to show the glory of God.

Indeed it is far from clear that the disciples were inquiring about reincarnation in the first place. It is more reasonable to assume that the question as to whether the man or his parents had sinned was a reference to the old doctrine that the sins of the fathers shall be visited upon the sons.

Other examples supporting reincarnation, drawn from the New Testament, are equally or even more farfetched. By careful selection and interpretation one can use the Bible to support practically anything. There is simply no reasonable evidence that Jesus or his immediate disciples were preaching reincarnation, or that the idea was even an issue at the time. But this is not to say that Christianity has never entertained reincarnation doctrines, for it very definitely has.

As Christianity began to make converts among the Greeks, or those influenced by Greek culture, as was practically every educated person of the time, Greek ideas began to seep into Christian doctrine. We have already seen that reincarnation was popular with some schools of Greek philosophy, and it was inevitably taken up by some Christian thinkers.

Undoubtedly the most influential early Christian supporter of reincarnation was the third-century teacher and martyr Origen. Origen was an enormously learned man, subtle thinker and prolific writer. His life was devoted to trying to work out some blending of Christianity and Greek thought. Among those ideas that Origen brought to Christianity from the Greek philosophers was reincarnation.

In one of his most famous treatises Origen wrote: "Is it not more in conformity with reason that every soul for certain mysterious reasons (I speak now according to the opinion of

Pythagoras and Plato and Empedocles, whom Celsus frequently names) is introduced into a body, and introduced according to its deserts and former actions? . . .

"Is it not rational that souls should be introduced into bodies, in accordance with their merits and previous deeds, and that those who have used their bodies in doing the utmost possible good should have a right to bodies endowed with qualities superior to the bodies of others?"

In another work he wrote:

"The soul has neither beginning nor end . . . Every soul . . . comes into this world strengthened by the victories or weakened by the defeats of its previous life. Its place in this world as a vessel appointed to honor or dishonor is determined by its previous merits or demerits. Its work in this world determines its place in the world which is to follow this . . ."

Though Origen had a large following among educated Christians, his ideas were by no means universally popular among all Christians. Indeed at times he was persecuted as severely by his fellow Christians as by the Romans, though he finally died as the result of ill-treatment received at the hands of the Romans. His works, however, continued to be debated, interpreted, misinterpreted, distorted, rewritten, and occasionally burned for several hundred years by friends and enemies alike.

When Christianity triumphed in the Roman world, all points of doctrine were not yet settled. Regularly during the first few centuries of the Roman Church, it appeared on the verge of splitting over some theological dispute. As often as not these disputes were only partly theological; politics and personality contributed mightily to the heat of the arguments.

In the year 553 an important council of the Church, meeting at Constantinople, pronounced an anathema or ecclesiastical curse on Origen's doctrine of the pre-existence of the soul and, by clear implication, on the doctrine of reincarnation, for in order to be "reborn" one must have existed at some earlier time. The words of the council were unmistakable. "If anyone assert the fabulous pre-existence of souls, and shall assert the monstrous restoration which follows from it: let him be an anathema." There followed several pages of examples, each example ending with the phrase "let him be anathema." It was strong stuff.

The Emperor Justinian, not content with the condemnation by the Church, issued his own anathema against the Origenan doctrine of pre-existence.

Why had both Church and Emperor come down so heavily on the doctrines of a theologian who had already been dead for two hundred years anyway? No one really seems to know. Justinian had first summoned the council in 543, and they had been meeting for a full ten years before they issued their anathemas against Origen. This was not unusual, for the bishops of the early Church were both argumentative and leisurely. Justinian himself was said to enjoy long complicated theological arguments.

But there are some odd things about these anathemas against Origen. When the council was first called, neither Origen nor the doctrine of pre-existence were ever mentioned. The concern appears to have developed later during the long debates. Pope Vigilius objected to the makeup of the council, which was heavily dominated by Oriental bishops, and refused to attend at all. There is considerable reason to suspect that a power struggle between Emperor and Pope, or some other complicated political maneuver, had more to do with the decisions of the council than the doctrine of pre-existence. It is even possible to make an argument that the anathemas were not really legitimate decrees of the council, and thus have no force in the Roman Catholic Church. The problem is almost unbelievably obscure.

Legitimate or not, the anathemas against Origen and the teaching of the pre-existence of the soul—and, by implication, reincarnation—had a powerful effect upon Christianity for centuries. Justinian's curse against anyone "who set forth these opinions together with their nefarious and execrable and wicked doctrine, and to whomsoever there is who thinks thus, or defends these opinions, or in any way hereafter at any time presumes to protect them" made any consideration of reincarnation at all a dangerous act.

So it was that for centuries, reincarnation, which had at least been a minority view in early Christian thinking, was blotted out entirely. Echoes of that ancient anathema can still be heard in modern times. Less than twenty years ago, a lot of religious people became very upset over a popular book about reincarnation. Many of the same people had accepted or at least tolerated the equally unscriptural practice of astrology.

But no idea can ever be completely obliterated. Some Christian sects that were condemned as heretical appeared to entertain reincarnation, as did a small number of unorthodox thinkers. The sixteenth-century Italian philosopher, Giordano Bruno, stated:

"I have held and hold souls to be immortal . . . Speaking as a Catholic, they do not pass from body to body, but go to Paradise, Purgatory, or Hell. But I have reasoned deeply, and, speaking as a philosopher, since the soul is not found without body and yet is not body, it may be in one body or in another, and pass from body to body. This, if be not [proved] true, seems at least likely, according to the opinion of Pythagoras . . ."

Bruno made this statement before the Inquisition. The Inquisitors were unimpressed and had him burned at the stake.

Now all of this talk of Origen and Pythagoras took place in a rarefied atmosphere occupied exclusively by philosophers and theologians. The common folk, if they knew about such disputes at all, would not have been interested in them. They had more practical and immediate concerns. Yet without the influence of Greek philosophy, they had their own reincarnationist ideas, some perhaps carried over from pre-Christian times.

One of the most common themes in folklore is that of the sleeping hero. This story held that some famous hero or king of the past had not really died but was merely "sleeping" and that someday he would awake to lead his people once again. The story in one form or another was generally most popular among people who had been conquered, and were longing for days of past glory.

Just such a legend was attached to King Arthur. In reality, Arthur had been a leader of the Britons, before their conquest by the Anglo-Saxons. The Arthur legend holds that the king had not been killed in battle but merely wounded, and that he had been carried off to the "Isle of Avalon," a legendary land of heroes, where he would sleep until the time came for the Britons to drive the Anglo-Saxons back into the sea.

The Arthur story was just that, a story, that people would tell to one another and write poems about. We don't even know whether many people really believed it, though later rulers of England were intent upon finding Arthur's body to prove that he was really dead, and not just asleep.

There are a number of reported occasions upon which a pretender, claiming to be some long dead hero or king awakened, or reborn, would gather a considerable following. Sometimes such movements became quite large and powerful. These "reincarnated" heroes were often madmen, who really believed what they said. In other cases the pretenders were conscious revolutionaries who merely adopted the name of the dead hero for political purposes.

Typical of such sleeping hero legends were those which collected around Frederick II, the brilliant and cruel Holy Roman Emperor of the thirteenth century. Frederick died suddenly in the year 1250. A monk reported that he had seen the Emperor descending into the bowels of the volcano Mount Etna, in southern Italy, while a fiery army of knights fell hissing into the sea. The monk had probably meant to imply that Frederick had gone to hell, for he had not been popular with the Church. But the common folk put an entirely different construction on this tale, for Mount Etna had long been regarded as the abode of sleeping heroes, including King Arthur himself.

Ten years after the death of Frederick, an impostor who lived on the slopes of Mount Etna and called himself Frederick II was able to gather a considerable following. The idea of a reborn Frederick did not last long in Italy, but it came up again and again in Germany.

In his book, *The Pursuit of the Millennium,* Norman Cohn describes some of Frederick's resurrections: "Thirty-four years after his death Frederick II underwent a resurrection . . . Under the year 1284 a chronicler tells of a former hermit near Worms who had been claiming to be the Emperor, and about the same time another tells of a similar personage who had been escorted into Lübeck amidst great popular enthusiasm. In both cases the pseudo-Frederick had vanished as soon as he seemed likely to be unmasked. Was it the same man who in 1284 succeeded in establishing himself in royal state in the Rhine valley? Perhaps not, for this last seems to have been not so much an impostor as a megalomaniac who really believed himself to be Frederick."

This impostor gathered a large following and challenged the living Emperor Rudolph. However, he was captured and burned at the stake. The pseudo-Frederick was apparently convinced, and convinced many of his followers, that he would rise from the dead. In fact, shortly after the pseudo-Frederick's death, yet another impostor appeared in the Low Countries claiming to be Frederick resurrected once again. He too was executed at Utrecht, but legends continued to proliferate around the pseudo-Frederick for centuries.

It was also quite common for individuals to claim that they were the reincarnation of some Biblical figure, usually one of the prophets. Typically, they predicted doom for the rulers. Such individuals too might also gather a considerable following, generally from among the poor and desperate who thought of them as God's agents sent to help them throw off the oppressors.

Both reborn heroes and prophets generally came to a bad end when they tried to overthrow the established civil and religious authorities with their proclaimed supernatural powers.

The common people rarely speculated much about the theological or philosophical problems raised by reincarnation. A large percentage of them merely accepted the possibility without question.

Reincarnation as a serious thought-out philosophy began to re-enter the mainstream of European thought during the Renaissance. By the seventeenth and eighteenth centuries such ideas had become almost respectable. Not only had the once-monolithic Church been splintered, but it was possible even to question whether Christianity, any form of Christianity, was the sole source of all truth. The writings of the ancients, particularly the Greek philosophers, were being rediscovered, and revered, and so were their occasionally reincarnationist ideas. Europeans also became increasingly aware of Eastern religions in which belief in some form of reincarnation was basic.

It would be a gross exaggeration to conclude that reincarnation was ever accepted by a majority of intellectuals in Europe and America. But it had become so acceptable in some circles that the nineteenth-century German philosopher, Arthur Schopenhauer, could write:

"Were an Asiatic to ask me for a definition of Europe, I should be forced to answer him: It is that part of the world which is haunted by the incredible delusion that man was created out of nothing, and that his present birth is his first entrance into life."

The British poet, William Wordsworth, wrote in his poem "Intimations of Immortality":

Our birth is but a sleep and a forgetting;
The Soul that rises with us, our life's Star,
Hath had elsewhere its setting,
And cometh from afar.

This poem was, and perhaps still is, required reading in high school literature courses. Though the poem does not specifically endorse reincarnation, it very definitely is a statement in favor of the pre-existence of the soul. That was the very doctrine that had been so roundly and thoroughly cursed by the Church in earlier centuries. People had once been burned at the stake for saying less than what Wordsworth said.

Throughout much of Western history, death has been viewed as grim and final. That is certainly the feeling expressed in these seventeenth- and eighteenth-century American tombstones.

Benjamin Franklin could even treat the once-forbidden idea quite playfully. At the age of twenty-two, he wrote his own epitaph. It was a bit premature, for he lived to be eighty-four. But as a young man he was so pleased with this bit of work that he often made copies for his friends.

The Body of B. Franklin,
Printer,
Like the Covers of an Old Book,
Its Contents Torn Out
And
Stripped of its Lettering and Gilding,
Lies Here,
Food for Worms,
But the Work shall not be Lost,
For it Will as He Believed
Appear Once More
In a New and more Elegant Edition
Revised and Corrected
By the Author.

Another group of Americans were not quite as lighthearted about reincarnation as was Ben Franklin. They were the nineteenth-century New England scholars, poets, and writers called the Transcendentalists. The movement was primarily made up of individuals who were seeking a new vitality in a religion that they felt had grown cold and meaningless. In order to do this they were willing to entertain a whole span of religious ideas, including many non-Christian ones. One of the ideas was reincarnation. Among the Transcendentalists there were people like Ralph Waldo Emerson, Henry David Thoreau, Bronson Alcott, and his daughter, the author, Louisa May Alcott. The group was never large, but it was very influential and it was eminently respectable. Ralph Waldo Emerson was not about to be burned at the stake, stoned, or even shunned for writing about reincarnation.

While the constant cycle of rebirth is looked upon as a pun-

Ralph Waldo Emerson

ishment in many Oriental religions, the Transcendentalists had a more optimistic view.

"It is the secret of the world that all things subsist and do not die, but only retire a little from sight and afterwards return again," wrote Emerson. "Nothing is dead; men feign themselves dead, and endure mock funerals and mournful obituaries, and there they stand looking out of the window, sound and well, in some new and strange disguise."

There is about all of the Transcendentalists' speculations an air of detachment. True enough, Thoreau wrote in his journals about having lived in Judea eighteen hundred years ago and ". . . as the stars looked to me when I was a shepherd in Assyria, they look to me now a New Englander . . . As far back as I can remember I have unconsciously referred to the experiences of a previous state of existence." But Thoreau was writing imaginatively; he was not seriously trying to present a case history of his life as an Assyrian shepherd. Reincarnation was not central to the beliefs of the Transcendentalists.

But it did become central to a different group of unorthodox religious thinkers, the Theosophists. Theosophy was founded by Madame Helena Petrovena Blavatsky, a woman who at best can be described as controversial. Her critics called her a lot worse, and, in truth, she was an unprincipled adventuress, an audacious fraud, and quite possibly insane too. She was altogether one of the most remarkable personalities this world has ever seen.

H.P.B., as she often called herself, was born in 1831 into a family of minor Russian nobility. While still a teen-ager, she married a middle-aged general, and promptly ran off with a British sea captain. For over twenty years H.P.B. roamed the world, supporting herself in a variety of ways, sometimes as a circus performer, but most often as a spirit medium.

In 1873, Madame Blavatsky came to New York, for America was the center of world spiritualism. She soon became a favorite of American spiritualists, occultists, and other seekers of strange and esoteric truths. While living in New York City she began a religion that she called Theosophy, though, naturally she claimed it was really a very ancient religion that she was just revealing. Theosophy itself went through a number of incarnations. It contained elements of spiritualism, European occultism and Kabalistic lore. But from its beginning it was influenced heavily by Oriental religions, particularly the Hindu religion, and this influence grew as Theosophy developed.

In 1876 Madame Blavatsky, having tired of the United States, sailed for India, where she seemed determined to undertake the impossible task of teaching Hinduism to the Hindus. She succeeded surprisingly well, not so much among the ordinary Hindus, but among the wealthy Indians and among the British residents of India. The Theosophical Society flourished in India, and its influence spread throughout Europe and back to America.

But there were problems. Any organization led by so mercurial a character as H.P. Blavatsky was bound to encounter problems. There were furious quarrels with associates, well-founded accusations of fraud, and from H.P.B. herself, hysterical threats to bring down the whole society if her authority was questioned. Finally she was hustled out of India, and sent to what everyone hoped would be quiet retirement in Europe. But quiet was not H.P.B.'s natural state. With the aid of some wealthy English Theosophists, she established what amounted to a rival society run from London, and upon her death in 1891, Theosophy split into several furiously warring factions. The war continues to this day, though fewer and fewer people are interested in it.

Madame Blavatsky's honesty, even her sanity, is not really the issue here. Though Theosophy had many detractors, it had a fair number of influential and intelligent supporters as well. The fact is that Theosophy stimulated a great wave of interest in Oriental religions, and particularly in the doctrine of reincarnation.

The Theosophists had their own version of reincarnation. They laid a heavy stress on the Eastern idea of Karma—that one could receive rewards, or suffer punishments, in this life for

Madame H. P. Blavatsky

good deeds, or sins committed in a past life. By Karmic Law they held that the justice of the universe could be brought into balance.

In her most famous book, *The Secret Doctrine,* Madame Blavatsky wrote: "It is only the knowledge of the constant rebirths of one and the same individuality through the life-cycle; the assurance that the same MONADS [roughly, souls] . . . have to pass through the 'Cycle of Necessity,' rewarded or punished by such rebirth for the suffering endured or crimes committed in the former life . . . it is only this doctrine, we say, that can explain to us the mysterious problem of Good and Evil, and reconcile man to the terrible and *apparent* injustice of life."

An innovative idea introduced by Theosophy was that reincarnation was evolutionary. Most Eastern religions hold that the aim of the soul is to escape from the Wheel of Rebirth, and to attain a state of Nirvana where the self ceases to exist. The Essenes spoke of the soul being "trapped" by the flesh, and being truly free only when not attached to a body. But to Theosophists each reincarnation was a fresh opportunity to move to higher and higher planes, or to more advanced evolutionary cycles. Just what these planes or cycles are to be is a bit obscure, and indeed the various Theosophical factions often disagree. But it is the idea of evolving through reincarnation that has proved such an attractive part of Theosophy. This doctrine was stated with unusual force and clarity by Anne Besant, Madame Blavatsky's most illustrious disciple:

"With reincarnation man is a dignified, immortal being, evolving towards a glorious end; without it he is a tossing straw on the stream of chance circumstances, irresponsible for his character, for his actions, for his destiny."

Currently both reincarnation and the Law of Karma are important parts of that strange collection of beliefs that has been called modern Witchcraft. Now the word "witch" immediately conjures up images of the Black Mass, Devil worship and a host of other horrific activities. Modern witches, however, are not the least bit horrific. They say that they are the followers of an ancient pagan nature religion, and that they have been persecuted and maligned throughout history because they stubbornly and heroically refused to give up their old gods and become Christians.

There is a good deal of dispute as to whether there ever really was an ancient Witchcraft religion at all. But there can be no dispute that today thousands upon thousands of people claim to be followers of such a religion. So, whether it existed in the past or not, it most certainly exists today.

To some outsiders, these witch beliefs look like a mixture of old folk traditions drawn from many sources and modern occultism. Many of the founders of modern Witchcraft were involved with British occultism during the early years of this century. They were well acquainted with the beliefs of the Christian Kabalists and the Theosophists. It seems likely, therefore, that reincarnation entered modern witch beliefs in this way. The witches, however, contend that such beliefs go back to ancient times.

Dr. Leo Louis Martello, one of the most outspoken of today's witches, places reincarnation at the very core of the witch religion:

"We believe in Reincarnation, in the Law of Karma, 'as ye sow so shall ye reap.' Or as the witch tenet goes: 'An ye harm none do what ye will. Do good and it will return threefold. Do evil and it will return threefold.' "

Another modern religion that places a heavy emphasis on a

form of reincarnation is Scientology. This religion is the creation of a former science-fiction writer named Lafayette Ron Hubbard. Hubbard began developing his theories in the 1950s, and today he heads a wealthy cult with thousands of followers throughout the English-speaking world.

Like Madame Blavatsky and the founders of many other religions, Hubbard has been the center of controversy for years. His finances have been the subject of particularly severe criticism, for Scientology has made L. Ron Hubbard a very rich man.

To non-Scientologists, Hubbard's theories are bizarre, inconsistent, often incomprehensible. Occasionally Hubbard sounds like he is writing parodies of himself. But none of this matters to the devoted Scientologist. The cult has survived criticism, ridicule, and legal challenges. It may even survive the death of its founder, just as Theosophy survived the death of Madame Blavatsky.

While Madame Blavatsky used (or misused, according to your point of view) the concepts and terminology of Oriental religion to explain reincarnation, Hubbard uses the language of the science-fiction writer. The soul in Hubbardian jargon is something called the Thetan. This immortal entity has inhabited many bodies, not always human ones. At one time, millions of years ago, says Hubbard, Thetans inhabited the form of clams. At another time the principal life-form was a different sort of mollusk called The Weeper. Thetans were sloths, apes, and finally *homo sapiens*.

What happens between existences? Writes Hubbard, "At death, the theta being leaves the body and goes to the between-lives area. Here he 'reports in,' is given a strong forgetter implant and is then shot down to a body just before it is born."

There are 'report areas' throughout the universe. A few exist on Earth but most apparently are on Mars.

Hubbard goes on to explore reincarnations not only on this earth but throughout the entire universe for trillions of years. One of the numerous oaths and agreements that Scientologists have to sign as they make their way upward through the cult's elaborate hierarchy is one in which they agree to abide by the rules and regulations of the organization on this planet and the universe "FOR THE NEXT BILLION YEARS."

Despite the terminology, there is nothing very new in Hubbard's concepts. They can be found, stated somewhat more elegantly perhaps, in Theosophy and in many Eastern religions. Scientology's "solution" is also not really original either. The promise Scientologists offer is that, through various techniques, an individual can become "Clear," that is, the Thetan or soul can be absolved of all of the bad things that happened to it in this and previous existences. This is very like the promise of Nirvana that forms the basis of the appeal of many Eastern religions.

Oddly, though, the Eastern religions currently popular in the West do not lay a particularly heavy stress on the concept of reincarnation. Groups like the Divine Light Mission, headed by the teen-aged "Perfect Master," Guru Maharaj Ji, and the Hare Krishna, with their robes and shaven heads, have authentic roots in Indian religion. Neither group denies reincarnation, but neither pays much attention to it. Reincarnation is much more important to religions like Theosophy, Scientology, and Witchcraft that are the creations of Westerners.

But most of us are not Theosophists, Scientologists, or witches, yet we too had heard of reincarnation, and perhaps think that there is "something to it." This belief or feeling is not usually based on the writings of some religious leader, ancient or modern, or on the speculations of philosophers. It is much more practical. We have been told that there are people who have somehow or other been able to recall their own past lives. In the next chapter we are going to examine just such recollections.

3

Reincarnation Casebook

In this chapter we are going to look at a half dozen "typical" reincarnation stories. Now I suppose that there is really no such thing as a "typical" reincarnation story, any more than there is a "typical" ghost story. While all of these accounts involve individuals who believe that they have recalled a past life or lives, the details vary greatly.

These stories are all modern, that is, they all occurred within the present century. They are all Western; the individuals involved are either Europeans or Americans. I am even tempted to say that all of the stories are true, but perhaps that is too strong an adjective. These six tales are not "true" in the sense that they provide solid proof that the phenomenon of reincarnation is a real one. The evidence presented here is far too scanty, too ambiguous, to draw any such sweeping conclusion.

Often there is only a single witness—the person actually telling the story. Sometimes the names in the stories have been changed to protect the identity of those involved so that it is quite impossible to check the accuracy of an account. Details are usually vague, and the interpretations made may be unjustified. There is no solid confirmation for any of these stories, and none is possible. These six stories would be thrown out of court as hearsay evidence. They would not be considered within the realm of scientific proof, for science demands a far higher quality of evidence than does the law. They fall into the class that scientists call "anecdotal evidence." With anecdotal evidence one can prove the existence of unicorns.

So the stories in this chapter are "true" only in the sense that they have been presented as real experiences, and many people have believed that they are real. They are typical of the score of accounts that are printed yearly in magazines and popular books about reincarnation.

The value of these stories, aside from the fact that they make interesting reading, is that they provide insight into the sort of accounts that modern believers in reincarnation use to support their beliefs. The believers argue that while the evidence in each individual case may have severe shortcomings, taken altogether they add up to an impressive argument for reincarnation.

There is some merit to this point of view. But one can argue the other way too. A lot of incomplete cases do not add up to a complete case.

The reader is, therefore, cautioned not to take these stories for any more than they are—intriguing but unsupported tales about a fascinating subject. In later chapters we will look in greater detail at some of history's most celebrated reincarnation cases in which a greater wealth of detail is available.

Alexandrina's Return

On March 15, 1919, five-year-old Alexandrina Samona died of meningitis. The death was especially tragic for her parents, Dr. and Mrs. Carmelo Samona of Palermo, Sicily, for the medical opinion was that Mrs. Samona could never have another child.

Three days after Alexandrina's death her mother had a dream in which the dead child appeared and said, "I have not left you for good. I shall come back again." A few days later she had the same dream again.

The following evening, as Mrs. Samona was repeating the story of the dreams to her husband, they heard three loud knocks at the door of the sitting room. The Samona's three boys had been expecting a visit from a relative and they ran to the door shouting, "Come in, Aunt Caterina!" But there was no one at the door.

At the urging of friends, the Samonas then visited a spirit medium. Spiritualism was popular in Italy at that time, and it was widely believed that mediums could put the living in contact with the spirits of the dead. During the séance the spirit of the dead Alexandrina did allegedly speak through the medium and confirmed that she was going to be reborn. The spirit told her mother that she had made herself appear in the dreams, that she had caused the knocks on the door, and that she would be reborn before Christmas "with you as my mother . . ."

At a later séance, Alexandrina indicated that her mother was going to have twins. Another voice speaking through the medium, who identified herself as a dead aunt of Alexandrina, said, "The child is quite right. She is trying to tell you that another entity, trying to return to earth, is with you now." Alexandrina talked of her hope of returning to her family with a sister.

The prospect of twins was bewildering to Mrs. Samona, who was quite sure that she couldn't have any children. But a gynecologist confirmed that she was five months' pregnant, and the probability was that she would have twins. For a while, though, it looked as if the prophecy delivered during the séance would never be fulfilled, for Mrs. Samona became ill, and there was grave concern that the result would be premature stillbirths. But she recovered, and on November 22, Mrs. Samona gave birth to twin girls.

The twins were markedly different from birth. One of them, who closely resembled the dead Alexandrina, was given that name; the second girl was named Maria-Pace.

As the twins grew, the differences between them remained, but the similarities between Alexandrina and her namesake became even more pronounced, in the opinion of her parents.

When the girls were about three years of age the case came to the attention of a popular Italian magazine, which ran an article about it. In that article Dr. Samona recounted the ways in which the two Alexandrinas resembled one another.

"Alexandrina, in short, continues to show a perfect resemblance to the deceased child. I can affirm in the most positive manner that in every way, except for the hair and the eyes, which are actually a little lighter than those of the first Alexandrina at the same age, the resemblance continues to be perfect. But, even more than on the physical side, the psychological similarity developing in the child gives the case in question further and greater interest."

Dr. Samona noted that both Alexandrinas were very calm, while Maria-Pace was lively and nervous. Both Alexandrinas had a strong aversion to cheese and to any kind of dirt, and both were left-handed, the only members of the Samona family that were left-handed.

The second Alexandrina did not appear to have any active memories of her former life, but occasionally she seemed to recognize certain places that she had not seen before. A striking incident occurred when the twins were about ten years old. They were being taken to the city of Monreale, where there was a famous old church, for the first time in their lives. Their mother remarked that they would see things that they had never seen before. But Alexandrina insisted that she had been to the place already. "Don't you recall that there was a great church with a very large statue of a man, with his arms held open, on the roof? And don't you remember that we went there with a lady who had horns and that we met with some little red priests in the town?"

Dr. Samona's account continues, "Suddenly my wife remembered that the last time she went to Monreale she had gone there with her little Alexandrina some months before her death, and that we had taken with us a lady of our acquaintance who had come up from the country for a medical consultation at Palermo, as she was suffering from disfiguring growths on her forehead, and also that just as we were going into the church we had met with a group of young Greek priests with blue robes decorated with red ornamentation. We also recalled that all these details made a deep impression on our little daughter."

Various articles about the case were published over the years in different European magazines. While the case was never really thoroughly investigated, reporters did obtain testimonials from a number of people who knew the Samona family and were familiar with the incidents surrounding the case of the two Alexandrinas. They confirmed the strange events which preceded the birth of the second Alexandrina, and the likeness of the girl to her dead sister.

And there the case rests. What is one to make of it? The easiest explanation, and the most probable, is that it is all the result of a series of odd coincidences made to seem supernatural by a family's quite natural desire to believe that they had never truly lost their daughter. But if you are inclined to believe in reincarnation, the case is at least suggestive.

"Here Is Where I Have Lived Before!"

Many of us have had the experience of entering a strange place and being struck by the feeling that we have been there before. This feeling, technically known as *déjà vu,* is usually brief and vague, and quickly forgotten. But sometimes it does not go away so quickly.

A young German woman had such an experience in 1967. The woman calls herself Inge Ammann, a pseudonym she adopted "to keep embarassing or scornful sensation seekers away." She first published a description of her experience in a German newspaper, and a translation of it has been reprinted in the anthology, *Reincarnation in the Twentieth Century*, edited by Martin Ebon.

The woman, aged twenty-six at the time of her experience, and her husband were taking a leisurely vacation drive across Germany. They had no specific destination and were content to take any route which appealed to them at the moment.

When the couple entered a town on the road toward Czechoslovakia, Inge Ammann found that it looked familiar, though she had never been there before. As they took a side road into a wooded area, this feeling grew stronger, until she cried out quite spontaneously, "Here is where I have lived before! I know exactly where everything is."

In a flash Inge Ammann became convinced that she had once been a peasant girl named Maria D. (as usual, the account does not give full names) and her parents had owned a farm near the town in the days before World War II. She could remember many details about the farm, the village, how her parents looked, and the fact that she had two older brothers. But she could remember nothing of her own death.

When she told her husband, he insisted that the whole thing was "crazy," and they had a terrible quarrel. But she could not be shaken in her belief, so finally they decided to drive back to the village. Her husband believed that when she was unable to identify places in the village she would shake her delusion.

Rather than being confused, Inge Ammann seemed able to identify everything. She noticed that the road had been resurfaced recently and that several of the buildings had new additions, but that in general the village had changed very little since the time that she had lived there in a previous life. She was able to show her husband around as if she were a tourist guide.

The couple went into the village tavern and Inge Ammann recognized the owner, though he had grown much older. Her husband started to question the tavernkeeper about the D. family, who were supposed to have been her parents in that past life. The tavernkeeper was at first unwilling to give out any information to a pair of strangers, but slowly, in a roundabout way, the story came out.

Both the parents were dead. One of the brothers had been killed during the war, the other was still alive and running the family farm. What about the girl Maria? The tavernkeeper said that she had died many years ago, quite tragically while she was still young. What had caused the child's death?

"Well," the man said, "it was an impossible sort of an accident. Maria had been inside the stable and she had been kicked by a horse . . ."

Upon hearing those words Inge Ammann turned pale, and screamed uncontrollably. She suddenly remembered the whole accident. "Once again I saw myself standing in back of the horse, walking towards it. And then the animal, suddenly startled, kicked wildly with its hind legs."

What is one to make of such a story? With its deliberately hidden details it is quite impossible to verify. It is not unjustified to assume that the whole thing is a piece of complete fiction. But it is not untypical of the kinds of stories cited to prove reincarnation.

"I Went to the Moon First"

The July, 1915, issue of *American Magazine* contained the recollections of a Minneapolis woman about her younger sister's reincarnation.

The girl, called Annie, was a half sister and fifteen years younger than the writer of the story. Annie had always seemed somewhat different from other children. She often appeared to know about things that a child of her age could not or should not have known.

When she was about four, Annie had an argument with her father and, like children do when they are angry, she announced that she was going to go away forever. Her father asked where she was going to go, "Back to heaven where you came from?"

The child shook her head and said quite calmly and seriously, "I didn't come from heaven to you. I went to the moon first, but —you know about the moon, don't you? It used to have people on it but it got so hard that we had to go."

For a moment it sounded as though Annie was about to spin one of her already familiar fairy tales. Her older sister got out pencil and paper to take it down. But she didn't tell the usual type of fairy tale at all.

She said, "I have been here [on earth] lots of times—sometimes I was a man and sometimes I was a woman."

When her father laughed at this statement the child became indignant and insisted, "I was! I was! Once I went to Canada when I was a man. I remember my name, even." When asked what her name had been she thought for a moment and said "Lishus Faber," though the words were not pronounced very clearly.

Her father, condescending a bit to play along with the game, asked what she had done for a living when she was in Canada.

Annie's response was, "I was a soldier and I took the gates!"

No one was quite sure what the phrase "I took the gates" meant and when the child was asked to explain, she merely repeated it, becoming more and more indignant because people didn't understand her.

The writer of this account was intrigued by her little sister's notion that she had lived in Canada in some previous life. She began to read about the history of Canada, hoping to find an incident in which somebody "took the gates."

Standard histories offered nothing of interest. Finally, in a rather quaint old book she found a brief account of the taking of a small walled city by a company of soldiers. The battle was of no great importance in the history of Canada, but it did represent a feat of considerable bravery on the part of the soldiers. One particular phrase caught the reader's attention, for it told of how a young lieutenant with his small band "took the gates."

The lieutenant's name was Aloysius LeFebre.

Yankees in Gray Uniforms

Hypnosis has often been used to induce recall of past lives. We will discuss the use of hypnosis in greater detail when we get to the celebrated Bridey Murphy case. Each year psychic and occult publications report dozens of cases involving hypnosis and reincarnation that do not receive the sort of attention that Bridey Murphy got. The case of George Field that was first given publicity in the December, 1966, issue of *Fate* magazine under the title of "Reincarnation of a Civil War Victim" is very representative of this genre.

Loring G. Williams was a New Hampshire high school teacher who practiced hypnotism as a hobby and entertained an interest in reincarnation. Williams had been trying to "regress" various subjects to recall past lives. He was particularly interested in finding a subject who could supply verifiable details about his or her past lives. This wasn't easy, because most subjects, even if they began talking about past lives, were so vague, or described times so remote from the present, that checking the details was impossible.

A fifteen-year-old neighbor named George Field, however, turned out to be a perfect subject. In the first place, he was extremely easy to hypnotize. And when in his hypnotic trance, he "remembered" a life as "Jonathan Powell," a farmer who had lived in North Carolina about a century ago. He was able to remember other details from Jonathan's life, such as his father's and grandmother's names and the name of the local minister. To Williams it first appeared that it was a story that could be easily and completely checked.

Williams directed "Jonathan" to describe the last day of his life. The hypnotized subject began to recount how he was loading potatoes for those "damnyankee soldiers." There was a quarrel because the soldiers were only going to pay a few cents per bushel for the potatoes, far less than Jonathan thought they were worth. He told of cursing the men in their "gray uniforms."

This point stopped Williams, for if they had been Yankee soldiers they should have been wearing blue, not gray, the color of the uniforms worn by the South. When the hypnotist queried Jonathan about this, he received the firm reply, "They ain't Southerners."

Jonathan was less concerned about the color of the soldiers' uniforms than about the fact that they were underpaying him for his potatoes. He told them to keep their damn money. Then he shouted, "Oh! They shot me! Those damnyankee soldiers shot me!"

The hypnotized teen-ager clutched his stomach and doubled up in apparent pain. The hypnotist quickly brought his subject back to the present.

During the hypnotic session George Field had talked of specifics. He mentioned the town of Jefferson in Ashe County, North Carolina, and that Jonathan Powell had lived there between 1832 and 1863. This was the sort of information Williams had been hoping to obtain for a long time. The existence of the town itself was quickly established, but other details had to wait until Williams could arrange a trip to North Carolina.

When the school session ended, Williams, his son Jack, and George Field loaded camping gear into a Volkswagen and headed for North Carolina. As the trio neared Jefferson, George claimed that he had definite "feeling" of having been there before. Williams put George into a hypnotic trance and, speaking as the long-dead Jonathan, he expressed utter dismay at how the town had changed.

A New Hampshire high school student recalled a former life in which he was a Southern farmer during the Civil War who had been shot by Yankee soldiers or renegades trying to steal his potatoes.

It was an encouraging beginning, but feelings do not represent much in the way of hard evidence. Williams was looking for material evidence to support Jonathan's claims. A visit to the county courthouse proved a disappointment, for it seems that no births or deaths had been recorded there before 1912. Property records were more helpful. The searchers found a copy of a deed of land conveyed to one Mary Powell in 1803. Jonathan had mentioned that his grandmother's name was Mary, and she would have been living at about that time. Powell was not a common name in the region.

Williams got a local historian to quiz Jonathan about events and personalities in the area at the time of the Civil War. The results were ambiguous, for while he seemed to know some things, there was much that he was completely unaware of.

Jonathan had mentioned a minister named Brown. No such minister was found for the area, but there were indications that a circuit-riding preacher named Brown had often come through Jefferson.

One of the most puzzling parts of Jonathan's narrative of his death was his description of Yankee troops wearing gray uniforms. A check of Civil War records indicated that there had been no Yankee troops in the Jefferson area at all during the war. But according to Williams, the local historian told him that there had been bands of renegades who had come down from the North from time to time to plunder the region. They may have worn stolen Confederate gray uniforms.

After the article on the case appeared in *Fate* Magazine Williams received a letter from a woman claiming that she was a distant relative of the Powell family. She confirmed the existence of a Jonathan Powell, something that Williams had been unable to do in his visit to North Carolina, and added a number of details about his life.

Williams continued to work with George Field, and in subsequent hypnotic sessions took him back to three lives previous to his incarnation as Jonathan Powell.

In the first he had been a girl who had led a miserable, starved existence at some unspecified time. When she was about twelve years old she was killed after being run over by a horse and wagon.

In a second, and equally dismal, existence George Field was also a girl. Here too the date was unspecified, but the subject described her death from disease in some detail. The symptoms of the fatal disease sounded to Williams very much like those of bubonic plague, the disease which swept Europe during the

Middle Ages, killing more than a third of the population.

In a third incarnation George Field talked of being a boy who worked on the docks and drowned when he was about fifteen.

The details for these other three lives were far less specific, and less checkable, than those supplied for Jonathan Powell. The most significant thing about them is that they were all so drab and undramatic. They are not the sort of lives that one would normally make up. Most of us prefer to imagine ourselves as Queens of Egypt, Renaissance noblemen, or soldiers in Caesar's legions if not Caesar himself. And yet short, brutalized, and unhappy lives were the lot of most people in history.

A Canadian Pioneer

Most of the reincarnation stories that surface every year receive no publicity, or get publicity only in the psychically-oriented magazines like *Fate.* But occasionally one gets wider publicity, as in the spectacular case of Bridey Murphy. A case that has quite recently received wide attention is that of a young Canadian woman named Joanne MacIver. If Joanne MacIver has not become the Bridey Murphy of the 1970s it is not for want of trying on the part of her enthusiastic supporters and publicists.

In 1962 amateur hypnotist Ken MacIver hypnotized his teenaged daughter Joanne and "regressed" her into a past life. Under hypnosis she claimed to be Susanne Ganier, who had been born somewhere around 1819 and lived on a farm near the village of Massie in northern Ontario.

Compared to most accounts of reincarnation given under hypnosis, Joanne MacIver's was richly detailed. She told of marrying one Thomas Marrow, a local farmer. After some years of marriage Marrow was accidentally stabbed to death by a pitchfork. Susanne lived on for many years, dying in 1903 at the age of eighty-four. She had no children.

The impressive feature of Joanne MacIver's reincarnation story is that she appeared to know a lot of things that she could not, or at least should not, have known. Joanne MacIver's present life was not that far removed, either in time or space, from the life attributed to Susanne Ganier. The MacIver family lived in Orillia, a small resort town eighty miles north of Toronto, and only one county distant from Massie where Susanne Ganier was supposed to have lived. But many of the details about the past life were exceedingly obscure points, not the sort of information that a teen-ager was likely to run across in the normal course of things.

For example, she related how she had lived in the village of Massie near Owen Sound. There was a village named Masse, a century ago, but it is no more than a crossroads today, and its name does not appear on most maps.

While Joanne's father was checking into the details of the story he located an octogenarian named Arthur Eagles who had lived in the area all his life. Eagles attested that when he was young he had known a Susanne Marrow, the widow of Thomas Marrow.

During the hypnotic session Susanne Ganier talked of sailing on Georgian Bay, around a jutting strip of land called Vail's Point. There is such a strip of land, named after an early settler. But the name is only used locally, and is not the sort of name that would be known to a nonresident.

Susanne Ganier also spoke of a friend of hers, a "Mrs. Speedie" who had been the postmistress in the nearby village of

Annan. MacIver located a tombstone for a Mrs. Speedie in the village of Annan. She died in 1909.

In this recital of evidence there is one obvious omission. Aside from an old man's recollections there is no documentary proof that a Susanne Ganier or Thomas Marrow ever existed. This is not altogether surprising, for in the nineteenth century northern Ontario was the frontier, and record keeping was poor. In addition MacIver says that there had been a fire in Owen Sound in the late 1800s, which would have destroyed any traces of such records that might have existed.

The case of Joanne MacIver first attracted the attention of Allen Spraggett, a writer for the Toronto *Star,* who has long been interested in psychic subjects, and has written a number of books in the field.

After Spraggett's articles came Dr. Ian Stevenson, probably the world's leading scientifically trained student of reincarnation. Dr. Stevenson himself hypnotized the girl, and was struck by the way in which she kept to the outlines of her story. He was convinced that there was no trickery involved either on the part of Joanne or her father, but farther than that he was not willing to go because of the lack of concrete evidence. He hoped to be able to investigate the case further, and that more evidence would turn up. We must mention that trickery must be considered in this case because the authentic details about Susanne Ganier's life could easily have been obtained, if someone had wanted to cook up a story.

Jess Stearn, another popular writer on the psychic, wrote a whole book entitled *The Search for the Girl with the Blue Eyes* (Joanne MacIver has blue eyes). While Stearn too attests to the honesty of all involved, and at least strongly implies that the case is an impressive argument for a belief in reincarnation, his book presents precious little in the way of solid new evidence, and leaves the reader curiously unsatisfied.

FAR MEMORY?

If a prize were being given for remembering the largest number of past lives, a sure competitor would be Joan Grant. She claims to remember more than thirty previous incarnations, and has made a living writing about them.

In a book called *Many Lifetimes* that Joan Grant wrote in conjunction with her psychiatrist husband, Denys Kelsey, she describes how it was to have so many past lives rattling around in a single consciousness.

"I was twenty-nine before I managed to recover the technique of being able to relive an earlier incarnation in detail and as a deliberate exercise. Until then, my conviction that I had had many lifetimes before I was born of English parents, in London on the 12th April 1907, was based on disjointed episodes from seven previous lives, four male and three female. These episodes, although as natural as memories from more immediate yesterdays, were frustrating, because I could not fill in the gaps in continuity which would have linked them into coherent sequences."

She simply assumed that everyone had the same sort of fragmentary memories of past lives that she possessed, but that people did not talk about these memories, because it somehow wasn't polite.

Joan Grant visited Egypt in 1935, and experienced a vague feeling of depression upon viewing the ruins of the ancient civilization. So much seemed to have changed. She was "surprised that certain avenues of trees no longer led from Hatshep-sut's temple to Karnak . . ." But the visit itself did not

The writer Joan Grant has claimed to recall some thirty previous lifetimes, including several in ancient Egypt.

trigger any great flood of memories about a past life in Egypt.

Eighteen months later, however, an apparently trivial incident did release just such a flood of memories. She was performing an experiment in psychometry with an ancient Egyptian scarab. Psychometry is the reputed ability to gain psychic information by simply handling an object. Mrs. Grant had already been interested in psychic subjects, before she became deeply involved in reincarnation. Handling the scarab was the key that unlocked a tremendous amount of information about her life in First Dynasty Egypt about 3000 B.C. She began dictating her memories of this past life and they ultimately resulted in a book called *The Winged Pharaoh,* which she calls a posthumous autobiography.

Mrs. Grant's ability to remember past lives is the result of a something she calls "far memory." "The technique of this type of far memory," she explains, "as opposed to the isolated incident which is a spontaneous recall or recovered with the aid of hypnosis, entails learning how to shift the level of the majority of one's attention from the current personality to the earlier one, while still retaining sufficient normal waking-consciousness to dictate a running commentary of the earlier personality's thoughts, emotions, and sensations."

She says that she first learned this technique during her incarnation as Sekeeta, the daughter of a First Dynasty Pharaoh and for a time the co-ruler of Egypt. Ancient Egypt, as described by Joan Grant, was a place where the psychic sciences and arts flourished. Far memory was one of these psychic sciences, one that Mrs. Grant asserts was especially useful to physicians. If the physicians could remember at least ten of their own previous deaths and rebirths, they could then reassure their dying patients that there was nothing to be afraid of.

The final examination for far memory in ancient Egypt consisted of a series of terrifying ordeals which had been "designed by her instructors to assure them that her insight would not be impaired by unresolved terrors from her long history." Among the ordeals was being locked in an underground chamber for four days and four nights, and a fight with a gigantic cobra that left such an impression that a fear of snakes had followed her down through the centuries.

A thousand years after Sekeeta's death she was reincarnated in Egypt once again as Ra-ab Hotep, an Egyptian nobleman who was leading a movement against the corrupt priests who had taken over the temples. This movement was called the Eyes of Horus, and resulted in a posthumous biography of that name.

Still other far memories were used by Mrs. Grant in other books, including *Return to Elysium,* a description of her life in Greece at the end of the second century B.C., when she was Lucina, the ward and pupil of a famous philosopher. In *So Moses Was Born* she returned once again to Egypt, this time in the court of Rameses II. In *Scarlet Feather* she was an American Indian warrior woman who had earned the right to wear a warrior's feathers by successfully undergoing the ordeal required of male warriors. Many of her other lives are less exciting and she says there is not much point in remembering them.

In 1958, Joan Grant met Dr. Denys Kelsey, a psychiatrist who also had a great interest in reincarnation. They realized that they "knew" each other from past lives: once as husband and wife in eighteenth-century England and, before that, in ancient Rome. At that time they had been an ill-matched pair. He was a young physician, she was a wealthy Roman matron much in love with him. He ignored her, so she committed suicide. In their twentieth-century reincarnations they are of more compatible ages and temperaments. They married, though she continues to write under the name of Joan Grant, a name from a previous marriage.

There is not a scrap of credible evidence that any one of the many past lives claimed by Joan Grant is the result of anything more than her vivid imagination. Her "far memory" books about the past are not taken seriously by historians. And yet they have been consistently popular. *The Winged Pharaoh,* which was first printed nearly forty years ago, is appealing to an entirely new generation of readers, a generation just as interested in reincarnation, it appears, as were their parents.

So there you have a half dozen "typical," "modern," "true" reincarnation cases. They differ widely in scope, from Joanne MacIver's modest recollections to Joan Grant's exotic adventures on the Nile. They involve hypnotic age regression, spontaneous recall, far memory, and even predictions of future incarnations. They are equally varied in evidential quality. Some, like Joan Grant's, one must either accept on faith or reject for lack of evidence. Others, like Joanne MacIver's or George Field's, appear to have bits of supporting evidence, but in neither case has the investigation been good enough, nor the evidence persuasive enough, to say that here is "proof" of reincarnation. They are tantalizing, intriguing, and perhaps because so many of us are willing to accept them, they tell us more about our own beliefs than about any past lifetimes.

Shortly we are going to examine, in some detail, a few of the best documented reincarnation cases in modern history. But before we do, we must make a short but necessary side trip into the animal world.

4

Transmigration

There has always been an undercurrent of belief in, or at least interest in, reincarnation in the West. But transmigration, that is, the incarnation of souls into forms other than human, has had very little support indeed during the last two thousand years.

One of the few who has speculated seriously on the subject was the American writer Henry David Thoreau. After visiting a menagerie, he wrote in his journal:

"What constitutes the difference between a wild beast and a tame one? How much more human the one than the other! Growling, scratching, roaring with whatever beauty and gracefulness, still untamable, this royal Bengal tiger or this leopard. They have the character and the importance of another order of men. The majestic lions, the king of beasts—he must retain his title . . . It is unavoidable, the idea of transmigration; not merely a fancy of the poets, but an instinct of the race."

Elsewhere in his writings Thoreau, musing about the condition of man, said:

"We have settled down on earth and forgotten heaven . . .

Henry David Thoreau

That Eternity which I see in nature I predict for myself also . . . Like last year's vegetation our human life but dies down to its root and still puts forth its green blade into eternity . . . Methinks the hawk that soars so loftily and circles so steadily and apparently without effort, has earned this power by faithfully creeping on the ground as a reptile in a former state of existence . . ."

Thoreau was writing more of a general feeling of unity with all of nature and all of life than of a transfer of souls. But this sort of feeling appears to be a necessary prerequisite for any serious belief in transmigration. Just this sense of cosmic unity underlies many Eastern religions in which the idea of transmigration is quite common.

In the West, however, evidence of a belief in transmigration is spotty and confusing. There are Pythagoras' disputed theories of transmigration. Beyond that there is a great deal of evidence that the Greeks at one time did believe that people could turn into animals, or even into plants. Greek mythology is filled with tales of human beings transformed into other shapes. While it seems highly doubtful that such beliefs carried much weight among the educated and cultured Greeks of the Golden Age during the fifth century, or among the Romans who later repeated the same tales, these stories were almost certainly based on much older folk beliefs.

In primitive societies even today, where people live close to nature, they identify themselves with animals. There is, for example, the totem animal, an animal that serves as a symbol for a particular family or tribe. And in back of this identification is the belief that their ancestors originally were this particular animal.

Transmigrations might take place during life, through a magical spell, or after death. One American Indian tribe believed that if one of their hunters was killed by a bear, then his soul would transmigrate into that bear.

Folk beliefs in transmigration, while by no means universal, appear to have been reasonably common throughout the world. Often they survived for centuries as superstitions or legends, no longer connected with the underlying religious sense of the unity of all living things, but as isolated beliefs.

As late as the end of the last century, people in the Faroe Islands, in the North Atlantic, were said to believe that the seals that landed there would appear in human form once a year. In

Cycle of transmigrations according to a Tibetan image

1872 an article in the journal of the Anthropological Institute, published in England, expanded upon this belief:

"The seals which abound on the rocky parts of the shore are regarded with profound veneration, and on no account could a native be induced to kill one, as they are said to be the souls of their departed friends. In the hut of the king is the skin of a large white seal, which I ascertained was piously treasured on account of having formerly been occupied by the soul of a maiden. The following is the legend related to me:

"Many years ago a beautiful young girl lived upon the island and was betrothed of a 'dacent boy' by the name of Rooney. One day Rooney and his bride-elect were fishing out in a coracle, when a storm arose and the frail craft capsized. The terrified lover endeavoured in vain to save his sweetheart. Before sinking for the last time she said farewell to him, and said she would become a white seal and would sing to him. The broken-hearted Rooney swam ashore, but his reason had fled. He daily made a pilgrimage round the island in the hope of meeting his departed in the shape of a white seal; but his journeys were always fruitless.

"At length one stormy winter night Rooney started from his couch saying, 'Hark I hear her singing. She calls me now,' and before anyone could stop him, he had bounded off and was lost in the darkness. His friends were about to follow when they were deterred by a plaintive voice, chanting a melancholy lay, but when daylight broke it ceased. Then a search was made and down on the seashore they found the dead body of Rooney with a dead white seal clasped to his breast."

Stories of this type, which are fairly common throughout much of the world, are generally found only in remote places in the West, or exist as half-remembered survivals from a very early time. The reason is that both Judaism and Christianity can not be reconciled with any sort of belief in transmigration. We have already seen how hard it is to reconcile the concept of reincarnation, the rebirth of the soul in different human bodies, with Judeo-Christian thought. Transmigration is far more alien.

To the ancient Hebrews, man was the product of special creation. He was made in the image of God and quite distinct from the lower animals.

"And God said, Let us make man in our image, and after our likeness: and let them have dominion over the fish of the sea, and over the fowl of the air, and over the cattle, and over all the earth, and over every creeping thing that creepeth upon the earth." (Gen. 1:26)

The Bible made it quite clear that man was something infinitely superior to the animals and distinctly different from them. Man had "dominion" over them. The Hebrews scorned people like the Egyptians who worshipped their gods in the form of animals.

So the concept that the human soul could somehow or other incarnate in the body of an animal was unthinkable. Animals were generally considered creatures without souls of any sort. This attitude was adopted by Christians, and carried on through the centuries without a great deal of debate. There were no subtle thinkers like Origen to speculate upon the possibility of transmigration.

But as we can see in the tale of the white seal, older folk beliefs managed to survive in a Christian environment, particularly among those who did not try to reason too deeply about their religion, and in areas where Christianity was incompletely absorbed. Probably the most widespread and best-known legends attached to transmigration are those of the werewolf.

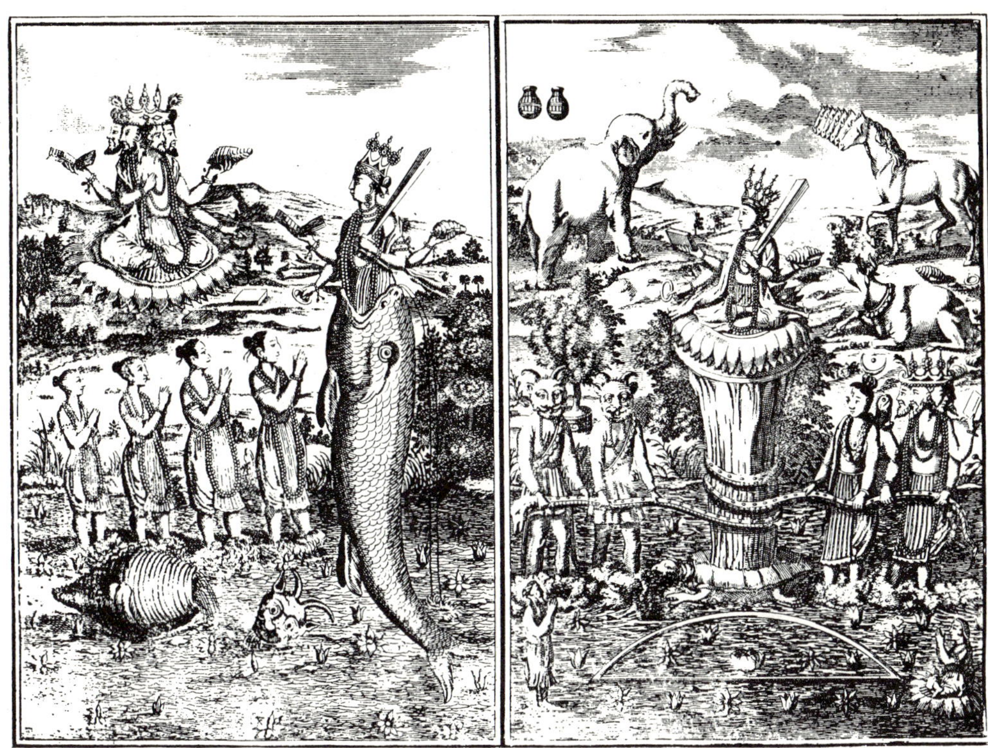

In Hindu mythology, the god Vishnu appears in various nonhuman incarnations, including that of a giant fish and a tortoise.

Commonly, werewolf stories concern living individuals who through some sort of magical means are turned into wolves. That type of belief falls outside of our area of examination, for we are concerned with human souls that incarnate into animal forms after death. There are a number of accounts in which the soul of a dead man, usually one who had been extremely evil during his lifetime, returns after death in a wolf form. This seventeenth-century story from Germany has been recounted by Frank Hamel in the book, *Human Animals.*

"The supposed incarnation of a dead burgomaster of that town [Ansbach] was said to be ravishing the neighboring country in the form of a wolf, devouring cattle as well as women and children. At last the ferocious beast was caught and slaughtered, and its carcass was encased in a suit of flesh-coloured cerecloth, while its head and face were adorned with a chestnut-coloured wig and long white beard, after the animal's snout had been cut off and a mask resembling the dead burgomaster's features had been substituted. This effigy was hanged, its skin stuffed and put in a museum, where it was pointed out as a proof of the actual existence of were-wolves. This incident appears to prove that the belief in were-wolves had been shaken at that date, but it has never been finally eradicated . . ."

Those accused of being witches in life were often thought to come back in the form of wolves or other animals after death unless certain precautions were taken. One of the precautions was driving a stake through the heart of the corpse. Modern fiction identifies this act exclusively with vampires, but historically it has been employed to keep any kind of restless spirit in its grave.

In some parts of Germany it was believed that one had to place money in the mouth of a corpse, at the time of burial, and cut the dead man's name out of his shirt; otherwise his ghost would rise from the grave in the form of a pig.

Churchmen were genuinely concerned about tales of were-wolves and ghostly pigs. They knew that such transformations were manifestly impossible in terms of scripture. The Bible stated quite unequivocally that God made all creatures of the earth "after his kind." To change that rule would take a miracle, and only God was capable of performing miracles. Since God would never create such a monstrosity as a werewolf, then the Devil must be responsible. But, the reasoning continued, the Devil could not turn a person into a real wolf, so the werewolf must be some sort of demonic illusion. The Devil was considered to be very good at creating illusions.

Learned monks wrote long and complex treatises on such subjects. These are no longer of interest to us today, but they do serve to indicate how completely antagonistic transmigration of any sort was to orthodox Christianity.

Less subtle thinkers grasped only half of the idea. They assumed that transformation was possible, and not just an illusion. But they also thought that it was exclusively diabolical. So, in Europe, the idea of transmigration became inextricably linked with demons, witches, ghosts, and a host of other concepts that it originally had nothing whatever to do with.

Throughout Europe there has always been a strong suspicion that certain individuals possessed the characteristics of different animals. There was a whole science, or pseudo-science to be more accurate, based on the theory of animal resemblances. If a man resembled a pig he was going to act like one, and so forth. The theory goes back at least as far as the ancient Greeks.

In Frank Hamel's book, *Human Animals*, a whole list of animal types is enumerated: "Most people are able to find physical similarities between human beings and animals. The equine man who moves his ears is not rarely to be met with. The person who uncovers his canine teeth in a snarl is an even more common type. Short women who flap their arms and waddle in the style of penguins; tall ones who have the graceful sliding movement of the giraffe; persons of either sex who jerk along with hops like feathered creatures on a lawn are all to be met with any day."

If the resemblance between a person and a particular animal is unusually strong, one may hear someone remark that the person must have been that animal in a previous life. But it appears that the real basis for the interest in animal resemblances lies in the ancient magical theory of analogy—if things are alike in one respect, then they must be alike in others—rather than in any deep belief in transmigration.

Sixteenth-century drawings illustrating the theory of human-animal resemblances.

Occultists, particularly those influenced by Eastern religions or magical theories which have their roots in ancient Greek thought, have given transmigration a more serious hearing than have orthodox Christians.

A very typical occult attitude is expressed by Marcia Moore and Mark Douglas in the book, *Reincarnation, Key to Immortality*:

"We should think twice before we mock the efforts of those eccentric people who devote an inordinate amount of time to their pets or fill their houses with stray animals. Not only are they helping to lighten an oppressive burden of bad karma [this important term roughly means the "debts" or "credits" that a soul accumulates in successive lifetimes; it will be discussed in more detail later] between the two kingdoms, but since there is evidence that more evolved animals also reincarnate, these pet lovers may be paving the way for the development of superior animal species in the future. They may also be assisting their beloved pets to leap the gap into the human stream of evolution when the door is again open between the two kingdoms. Occultists call the path between the animal and human kingdoms 'The Bridge of Sighs,' while the path between the human and superhuman kingdoms is called the 'Rainbow Bridge.' They claim that at certain times the traffic along these ways increases while at other times it is virtually cut off. During this era of history the higher way to the fifth or supra-mental kingdom is opening, but the lower bridge is closed, since humanity already has enough undeveloped egoes with which to contend."

Probably no one in modern times developed this idea of souls passing between various "kingdoms" more completely, or produced a more complicated and exotic picture, than Helena Petrovena Blavatsky, founder of Theosophy. As part of her elaborate cosmology she "revealed" the seven Root Races through which the soul or Monad incarnated in its progress toward the infinite. The First Root Race appeared to have been a sort of astral jellyfish. The Second lived on the lost Arctic continent of Hyperborea. The Third were gigantic, apelike egg-laying Lemurians. The Fourth Root Race were the Atlanteans. We are the Fifth Root Race, and the Sixth is about to appear.

At least this is what Madame Blavatsky seems to be saying. But her theories are not always consistent, and her prose often unfathomable, as a brief quote will show:

". . . it is most important to remember that the Egoes of the Apes are entities compelled by their Karma to incarnate in the animal forms, which resulted from the bestiality of the *latest* Third and the earliest Fourth Race men. They are entities who had already reached the 'human stage' before this Round. Consequently they form an exception to the general rule. The numberless traditions about Satyrs are no fables, but represent an extinct race of animal men. The animal 'Eves' were their foremothers, and the human 'Adams' their forefathers; *hence the Kabalistic allegory of Lilith or Lilatu*, Adam's *first wife*, whom the Talmud describes as a *charming* woman with *long wavy hair*, i.e., a female hairy animal of a character now unknown, still a female animal who, in the Kabalistic and Talmudic allegories is called the female reflection of Samael, Samael-Lilith, or man-animal united, a being called *Hayo Bischat*, the Beast or Evil Beast (Zohar) . . ."

This quote is reasonably typical, so it is little wonder that Madame Blavatsky's books have a limited readership outside the devoted circle of Theosophists.

The occultists in the West have taken the idea of transmigration to heart, but they have so complicated it with such a host of other theories and speculations that it is hard to figure out what they are talking about.

From time to time I have heard of individuals who are said to have seriously believed that their pet dog or cat was the incarnation of a human being, often a dead friend or relative. But I have never actually met anyone who contended this; all the stories I have encountered are second or thirdhand. They may involve people who are mentally unbalanced, or they may be made up entirely.

Fiction is the place where the best tales of transmigration can be found. The English short-story writer, Saki (H. H. Munro), produced a marvelous little transmigration tale called "Laura." Laura is dying, and she explains to her friend Amanda that since she has not been very good in this life she expects to come back in the next life as some sort of animal.

"'You see,' resumed Laura, 'I really *have* some grounds for supposing that my next incarnation will be in a lower organism. I shall be an animal of some kind. On the other hand, I haven't been a bad sort in my way, so I think I may count on being a nice animal, something elegant and lively, with a love of fun. An otter, perhaps.'

"'I can't imagine you as an otter,' said Amanda.

"'Well, I don't suppose you can imagine me as an angel, if it comes to that,' said Laura.

"Amanda was silent. She couldn't."

Laura dies, and a few weeks later an otter shows up in the stream of Amanda's garden. The animal is so destructive that despite Amanda's misgivings a hunt is organized for it. The results of the hunt are explained to Amanda by a friend.

"'Did you—kill?' asked Amanda.

"'Rather. A fine she-otter. Your husband got rather badly bitten in trying to 'tail it.' Poor beast, I felt quite sorry for it, it had such a human look in its eyes when it was killed. You'll call me silly, but do you know who the look reminded me of? My dear woman, what is the matter?'"

And, finally, what may well be the silliest use of the transmigration theme in all history turned up a few seasons back as the basis of a television show. It was about a young man whose mother was reincarnated as a car. The title of the show was "My Mother the Car." It failed quickly.

While the subject of transmigration has not been taken seriously in the West for quite a long time, there is a possibility that that might change. Eastern religions are attracting an increasing number of Western converts. More significant, though, is the growth of what might be called the ecology ethic—the idea that man is part of nature and must live in harmony with it. This is a rejection of the Old Testament statement that man has domination over all other living things. As we pointed out at the beginning of this chapter, a sense of unity with all nature is a necessary prerequisite for any serious belief in transmigration. Whether the spread of such ideas ultimately will lead to an upsurge of interest in transmigration, only time will tell, but the groundwork at least is there.

5

From India to the Planet Mars

On March 10, 1895, a group gathered in a drawing room in Geneva, Switzerland, watched a most remarkable and chilling sight. A thirty-year-old Swiss woman named Catherine Elise Muller, but known to posterity as Hélène Smith, rose from the table at which she had been sitting entranced for nearly an hour, and began to play out in pantomime a scene in which a Hindu princess of the fifteenth century is burned to death on her husband's funeral pyre.

An eyewitness to the scene gives this description:

"She goes slowly around the room, as if resisting and carried away in spite of herself, by turns supplicating and struggling fiercely with those fictitious men who are bearing her to her death.

"All at once, standing on tiptoe, she seems to ascend the pile, hides, with affright, her face in her hands, recoils in terror, then advances anew as though pushed from behind. Finally she falls on her knees before a soft couch, in which she buries her face covered by her clasped hands. She sobs violently . . . It is the moment at which she again passes through her agony on the funeral pile: her cries cease little by little; her respiration becomes more and more panting, then suddenly stops and remains suspended during some seconds which seem interminable. It is the end!"

A previous incarnation as the Indian princess Simandini was only one of Mlle Smith's many psychic feats. She had at another time been Queen Marie Antoinette of France. She also visited the planet Mars to speak to the Martian reincarnations of her friends. Later in life she took to describing herself as a reincarnation of Mary.

While playing out her reincarnated lives, Mlle Smith was also often in touch with the spirits of others long dead, including some very famous individuals. Her first spirit guide was the great French writer Victor Hugo. Hugo, however, was soon displaced by a more powerful and mysterious figure called Leopold. Ultimately Leopold revealed his true identity as that of Joseph Balsamo, an eighteenth-century Sicilian occultist, adventurer, and swindler known best under his adopted name, the Count of Cagliostro. (Actually his name was not Joseph but Peter Balsamo, though most people then as now called him Joseph.)

Often it was difficult to know just who was in control of the woman's body at any given time. While she was acting out Simandini's death scene, Leopold retained control of the little finger of her right hand. He continued to tap out answers to questions being asked him, quite independently of the state of the rest of Hélène Smith's body. That in itself must have been eerie to observe.

While the many lives of Hélène Smith are bizarre, she is not entirely unique in history. What makes her case an exceptionally valuable one is that we know so very much about it. Early

Cagliostro

in her career Mlle Smith met Theodore Flournoy, a well-known professor of psychology at the University of Geneva. Flournoy studied her case closely over a number of years, and was regarded by Mlle Smith not only as a friend but also as the reincarnation of her fifteenth-century Indian husband Prince Sivrouka Nayaka. Flournoy gave the woman the pseudonym of Hélène Smith and his book on the subject, called *From India to the Planet Mars,* is one of the most complete and fascinating ever written on such a case. After Professor Flournoy departed the scene, another psychologist, Professor Deonna, kept track of Mlle Smith's many lives up until the time of her death in 1930. The record of her life or lives is unusually complete.

Hélène Smith came from a modest, but very respectable family. Her father was an emigré Hungarian, her mother a Swiss. Hélène had always been a quiet, timid, and rather dreamy child. Early in life she had taken up embroidery, at which she became quite skilled, and she produced bizarre and original works.

As a child she had an imaginary playmate, and could remember several occasions when she believed she had been rescued from danger by some sort of a benevolent but invisible spirit.

While not everyone has such feelings and experiences during childhood, they are reasonably common. In any case, by the time she had reached the age of twenty these imaginary playmates and guardians had disappeared from her life. Nor did the once-dreamy child become a recluse—quite the contrary. She held a difficult and responsible job in a large store where she was known as an exceptionally hard and effective worker.

Hélène Smith was a large woman, and everyone who met her was impressed by her robust good health, and tremendous energy. She was also characterized by a certain aloofness, even snobbishness, a feeling of being somehow better than those around her. She had never married, apparently because she had never found anyone good enough for her. While she attended scrupulously to all her family and business duties, she had always felt out of place in the world of middle-class Geneva.

Even after she began to reveal her other lives in India, Mars, and the royal palace of France, Mlle Smith did not appear outwardly odd in any way. Wrote Flournoy, "I was about to say that in her normal state Mlle Smith is normal. Certain scruples restrain me, and I correct myself by saying that in her ordinary state she seems just like anybody else . . . no one would suspect, observing her performance of her various duties, or in talking with her on all sorts of subjects, all that she is capable of in her abnormal states . . .

"With a healthy and ruddy complexion, of good height, well proportioned, of regular and harmonious features, she breathes health in everything. She presents no visible stigmata of degeneration. As to psychic defects or anomalies, with the exception of her mediumship itself, I know of none, the timidity of her youth having entirely disappeared. Her physical strength is marvellous . . ."

Mlle Smith had an excellent memory which helped her greatly in her job where she had to keep track of an endless stream of details. But her memory often operated in a rather odd way. Flournoy gave an example of an occasion when a clerk asked Mlle Smith what had happened to a particular pattern. She replied without thinking, "Yes, it was sent to Mr. J." (a customer of the firm). As she was replying the number 18 appeared before her in large black figures nearly a foot high, so she added, "It was eighteen days ago."

That answer caused the clerk to smile, for it was a firm rule of the store to lend out patterns for only three days. If a customer kept a pattern longer a messenger was sent to get it. The clerk reminded Hélène of the policy, and since she had no conscious recollection of how long the pattern had been gone she agreed that perhaps she had been wrong.

But when the store records were checked it was discovered that she had been quite correct. The store had failed to retrieve the pattern from Mr. J. through a series of minor oversights with which Mlle Smith had nothing whatever to do. She had doubtless learned about the oversights during the course of her work, but the information had not registered on her conscious mind. Rather it had sunk into her unconscious, and was brought back to her consciousness in a strange but dramatic way.

Sometime during the winter of 1891–92 Hélène Smith was introduced to the practice of spiritualism by an acquaintance. Spiritualism was fairly new in Switzerland at the time, and there as elsewhere in Europe it had become all the rage. The practice had started in America in 1848. Groups of people would gather together for a séance, a meeting held to make contact with the spirits of the dead.

In order to have a successful séance one of the group had to be a medium, that is, someone who is specially "gifted" to be an intermediary between the world of the living and the spirit world. With a medium present the spirits might communicate in a variety of ways: moving a table or rapping in code, by speaking in a disembodied voice, or actually appearing "materialized."

More commonly, though, the spirits were supposed to take control of the medium's body and use it as an "instrument" for communication, either by actually speaking through the medium or guiding her hand (most but by no means all mediums were women) in automatic writing.

Many mediums, particularly those who produced the physical phenomena—materializations, moving tables, and the like—were frauds. For the mental mediums, those who were possessed during the séance, the problem of deciding who was a fraud is not such an easy one. The medium who put on a sheet dyed with a luminescent substance and ran around the room claiming to be the spirit of someone's long dead grandmother was a fake, and knew it. The medium who went into a trance during a séance and then spoke, claiming to be the spirit of the dead grandmother, might or might not be a fraud. But even if she was not a faker, that does not mean the message was an authentic communication from the dead woman, or from anyone or anything outside of the medium herself.

This is the problem that we face with Hélène Smith. Though she was closely investigated for years, there was never a suspicion that she was a conscious fraud, that she ever made up any of the things she said during her séances in order to fool people.

A few mediums had come to doubt their own sanity. They wondered if all of these messages that suddenly erupted from their mouths when they went into a trance were signs of madness. One famous medium practically devoted her life to being studied by the Society for Psychical Research. She didn't do it for money, for she received practically nothing, but rather she said to find out if she was "possessed or obsessed," that is, to find out whether the influences which took hold of her during séances came from without or within.

Hélène Smith had absolutely no doubts that her messages came from spirits or entities outside of her own body. She strongly and angrily rejected even the slightest suggestion that there could be anything abnormal about her. Said Flournoy, "She declares emphatically that she is 'perfectly sane in body and mind, not in the least unbalanced,' and repels with indignation the idea there can be any serious abnormality or the least danger in mediumship such as she practices. 'I am far from being abnormal,' she wrote me recently, 'and I have never been so clear of vision, so lucid, and so apt to judge correctly as since I have begun to develop as a medium!' "

When Mlle Smith first began attending séances she was not a medium, and apparently had no intention or thought of becoming one. But very quickly odd phenomena began to manifest themselves. By her second séance she had begun to show signs of automatic writing. A few séances later she was seeing bright lights, and after two months she reported the presence of the spirit of the writer Victor Hugo as her guide and protector.

A more disturbing thing also happened, according to the account of one who attended the séance. "She is very restless, and sees suddenly, balancing itself above the table, a grinning, very ill-favored face with long red hair. She is so frightened that she demands that the lights be lit."

Victor Hugo turned out to be a passive and rather unsatisfactory spirit guide, and by early 1892 Mlle Smith's séances were often interrupted by the presence of a more powerful but hostile spirit called Leopold. Mlle Smith described him as being a man of about thirty-five, all dressed in black. During one séance Leopold was supposed to have pulled Mlle Smith's chair from under her twice, causing her to injure her knee. Slowly but

The handwriting of Leopold as written by Mlle Smith incarnating as this eighteenth-century figure (above), compared to the normal handwriting of Mlle Smith (below left).

surely Leopold began to take over the séances and Victor Hugo disappeared.

As Leopold's power over Mlle Smith grew, his personality began to change. Instead of being a hostile spirit, he was slowly transformed into a guardian spirit, who not only appeared at séances, but at other times in her life as well. As a child Hélène had been attacked by a large dog while walking home from school. Quite suddenly a man in a long brown robe, with flowing sleeves and wearing a white cross on his breast appeared and chased the dog away. The robed man left before she had a chance to thank him. Flournoy believed that such an incident actually had taken place, and impressed itself strongly on the child's mind. Her parents recalled her talking about being saved from a dog at the time. Later, from time to time, this same brown-robed figure had appeared to Mlle Smith in order to guide her away from some unpleasant sight or dangerous encounter. These later meetings Flournoy believed to be visions or hallucinations.

Though Leopold first revealed himself in séances wearing a black robe, he said that he was also the brown-robed guardian of Mlle Smith's childhood. She accepted the identification instantly.

When Mlle Smith was discussing Leopold with some spiritualist friends, one told her that he sounded just like the spirit of Joseph Balsamo, the infamous though bogus Count of Cagliostro. Cagliostro, who had lived during the eighteenth century, was very much in vogue with nineteenth-century occultists and spiritualists, especially after he had been used as a leading character in a popular historical romance. Cagliostro was also widely believed to possess all sorts of occult or psychic gifts. Soon after discussing Cagliostro with her friends, Leopold told

Mlle Smith that he was really Cagliostro. However, he continued to use the name Leopold much of the time.

For a while Mlle Smith considered herself to be the reincarnation of Lorenza Feliciani, Cagliostro's beautiful wife. Then she found out that the real Lorenza was not at all like the Lorenza of the novel, and in fact not a very admirable character. So she abandoned the Lorenza idea. I must stress that her belief that she was Lorenza was a conscious one, not something that had come out while she was in a trance.

Reincarnation was not central to spiritualism, though many spiritualists certainly believed in it, and more were willing to at least entertain the possibility than were orthodox Christians. A medium who, while in a trance, took on the personality of a past life was called an "incarnating medium." This was considered an advanced form of mediumship, to those who believed in spiritualism, or a more serious form of mental illness to those who did not. The medium was no longer taken over temporarily by a spirit, the medium actually *was* that spirit.

Up to the winter of 1894–95, when Mlle Smith met Professor Flournoy, she had not been an incarnating medium, though she often revealed the identities of previous lives of other sitters in the séance. The lives in India, Mars, and as Marie Antoinette did not develop until later, and Flournoy believed himself to be at least partly responsible for this development. "I fear," he wrote "that this change must in great measure be attributed to my influence, since it followed almost immediately upon my introduction to Hélène's séances."

Of her three major incarnations during this period, Hélène's incarnation as Marie Antoinette, the tragic Queen of France, is easiest to understand and to explain. As we have already noted, Hélène had always felt "too good" for the humble surroundings in which she had been born. What then is more likely than an identification with royalty, and particularly with Marie Antoinette, who was at the time a popular figure of romantic fiction?

There is another connection too. A widely read novel by Alexander Dumas closely linked Cagliostro with the Queen. In fact, the two may have known one another. But their relationship was not close, for Cagliostro had never truly penetrated the inner circle of court society, although he tried to pretend he had. In any case, the association was widely believed, and Mlle Smith had been known to discuss it with friends.

After first toying with the idea of having been an incarnation of Lorenza Feliciani, Cagliostro's wife, Mlle Smith soon revealed herself in a séance as the incarnation of the Queen. It was an identification with which she was clearly more comfortable.

As Marie Antoinette, Hélène Smith would often act out scenes from the Queen's life. But, as in the Indian scene described at the beginning of this chapter, the spirit of Leopold still controlled her little finger, and by finger signals Leopold would describe the scene that the Queen was acting out.

While incarnating as Marie Antoinette, Mlle Smith also wrote messages. Her handwriting at such times differed considerably from her normal handwriting but it did not compare in any significant way with the known handwriting of the historical Marie Antoinette. Interestingly, though, comparisons between messages allegedly written under the influence of Leopold/Cagliostro, and handwriting samples of the real Cagliostro, were much closer.

Occasionally Marie Antoinette would intrude into Mlle Smith's waking life. One night Flournoy was taking her home

Vos lignes sont charmantes
mais vos façons mystérieuses
le sont-elles autant
J'étois cependant prévenue
depuis une huitaine que l'on
préparoit votre maison et qu'il

Comparisons of the writing of Mlle Smith incarnating as Marie Antoinette (above) and the writing and signature of the real Marie Antoinette.

et du courage, mais l'intérêt de mon fils est
le seul qui me guide et quelque bonheur que
j'eusse éprouvé à être hors d'ici je ne peux pas
consentir à me séparer de lui au reste je
reconnois bien votre attachement dans tout ce que
vous m'avez détaillé hier; comptez que je sens la bonté
de vos raisons pour mon propre intérêt, et que cette
occasion peut ne plus se rencontrer, mais je ne pourrois
jouir de rien en laissant mes enfans et cette
idée ne me laisse pas même de regret.

Marie Antoinette

after a séance in which she had spent much of the time as the Queen. She suddenly expressed the strong desire to be taken to the house of a well-known person who had been received at the court of Marie Antoinette, and who had died in Geneva about seventy-five years earlier. Only when Mlle Smith, with Flournoy in tow, actually arrived at the house and got ready to enter did she return to herself. As usual, she remembered nothing of what had happened and was very surprised to find herself in this unaccustomed place.

Often nineteenth-century words like telephone, bicycle, and steamship slipped into the Queen's eighteenth-century conversation. At times other characters who took control of Mlle Smith during these periods tried to trap the Queen into uttering such inappropriate words, and took a malicious delight when she stumbled. Says Flournoy, "Marie Antoinette first allows the treacherous word to pass unnoticed, and it is evident that she perfectly understood it, but her own reflection, or the smile of the sitters, awakens in her the feeling of incompatibility; she returns to the word just used, and pretends a sudden ignorance and astonishment in regard to it."

The fact that Mlle Smith found herself transported to the planet Mars during séances may seem rather odd to us. We tend to think that the idea of life on other planets and space travel is entirely a modern development, and that people at the end of the last century didn't bother about such ideas. But spiritualists had often discussed the possibility of life on other planets, and Hélène Smith was not the first medium to bring back messages from outer space. In 1877 the astronomer G. V. Schiaparelli announced the discovery of "canals" on Mars, and that planet had excited a great deal of interest and speculation. Hélène Smith was known to have been interested in the subject.

Late in 1894 Mlle Smith was trying to contact the spirit of a young man named Alexis Mirabel who had died some years earlier. His mother was at the séance. The medium found herself being transported through space to a strange, but beautiful place. "On what am I walking?" she asked. By raps the table replied in code, "On a world—Mars."

Flournoy, who witnessed the séance continues: "Hélène then began a description of all the strange things which presented

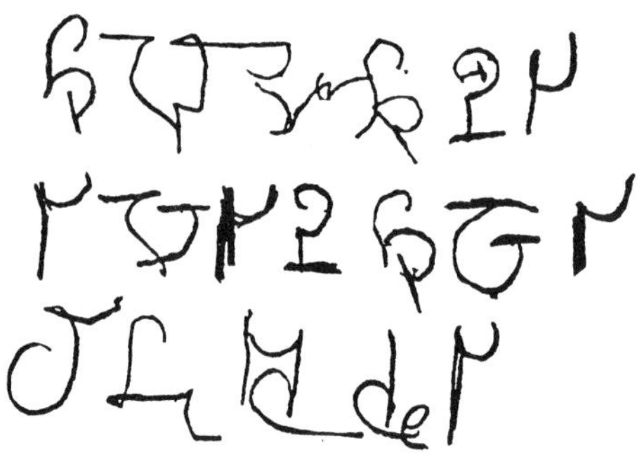

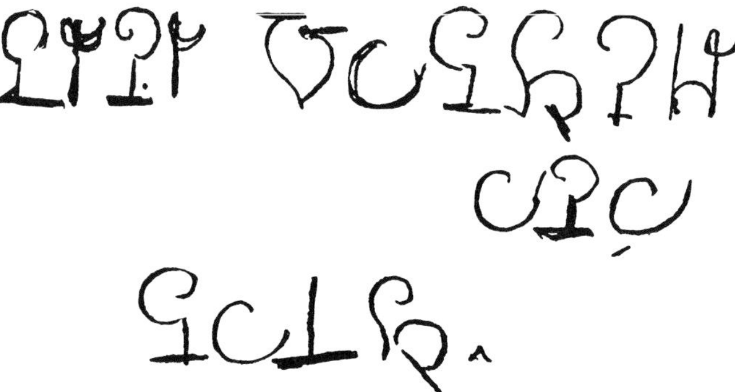

Examples of the Martian language (above and opposite) as written by Hélène Smith

themselves to her view, and caused her as much surprise as amusement. Carriages without horses or wheels, emitting sparks as they glided by; houses with fountains on the roof; a cradle having for curtains an angel made of iron with outstretched wings, etc. What seemed less strange were people exactly like the inhabitants of our earth, save that both sexes wore the same costume, formed of trousers very ample, and a long blouse, drawn tight about the waist and decorated with various designs."

In her visions the medium located Alexis Mirabel, for he had been reincarnated as a Martian. He offered his mother the same sort of soothing words that spirits in séances always seem to offer grieving loved ones. He also gave her suggestions for treating an eye disease from which she happened to be suffering.

Hélène Smith returned to Mars again and again during her

séances and she built up a complex, and surprisingly consistent, picture of life on that planet. There were regular characters in her visions. The leading one was Astane, a learned man, who was supposed to be a reincarnation of someone that Mlle Smith had known in a previous life. Other Martians were reincarnations of sitters at the séance or of other acquaintances. Hélène Smith herself did not appear to have a clear Martian incarnation. She generally reported on doings there as a visitor, or allowed the spirits of the Martians to "control" her body. She did not "become" a Martian.

Mlle Smith not only described the Martian scene, but drew pictures of it and of some of the leading characters in the stories she told. The pictures, while rather exotic looking, do not look all that different from earthly scenes. They look most like illustrations for a nineteenth-century children's book of Oriental tales.

What was most impressive about the Martian Cycle, as Flournoy called this phase of the medium's career, was her use of a "Martian language." In a séance held February 2, 1896, Leopold informed the sitters that Hélène Smith was going to address them in Martian. One of the sitters tried to take down what she said as accurately as possible.

"Mitchma mitchmon mimini tchouainem mitatchineg masichinof mezavi patelki abresinad navette naven navette mitchichenid naken chinoutoufiche . . ." Her voice grew louder and her speech more rapid and soon it became impossible to transcribe her words at all. At that séance and others that followed, the medium had a good deal more to say in the Martian language.

For thousands of years we have witnessed the phenomena of glossolalia or "speaking in tongues." It is mentioned in the

Bible as one of the "gifts" of early Christians. Individuals, usually in the grip of an intense emotional or religious experience, will suddenly burst out speaking or singing in what sounds to them, and others, like an unknown language. Glossolalia may sound like Latin to a person who speaks no Latin, Chinese to an American, or possibly English to a Chinese. Some people who realize that these sounds are no known language say that they represent the "tongues of angels."

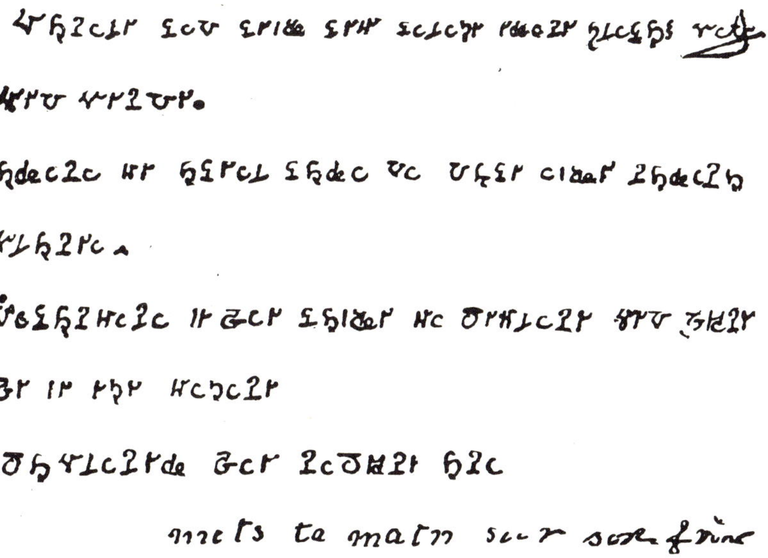

At the very end of this Martian text the character of Leopold takes over and begins writing in French.

Psychologists who have studied glossolalia—and the subject has been studied extensively—contend that it is not any sort of language known or unknown. Rather it is a string of meaningless sounds, given the appearance of language by being broken up by the speaker into what sounds like words and sentences. Glossolalia, say the psychologists, expresses a general emotional state rather than any specific ideas, and one compared it to improvisational jazz rather than language.

Hélène Smith, however, did not merely speak in tongues, she wrote in tongues as well, and what is more, she wrote in unknown characters. When entranced she would set down lengthy messages in the Martian language. It turned out that her glossolalia was not just a string of meaningless sounds, or incomprehensible scribbles. It was consistent, and could be translated. It was a language.

But it was obvious when the language was translated that the medium had used the French language, her native tongue, as the basis for her Martian language. For example, the Martian word for "no" is *ke ami*, while the French word for "no" is *ne pas.* The syntax and grammar were also based on simple French. Most of us could, if we put our mind to it, invent a similar language. What was so impressive about Mlle Smith's performance was that this was all accomplished unconsciously. She could consistently speak or write long passages in this language, without having ever practiced it. Most glossolalia is free

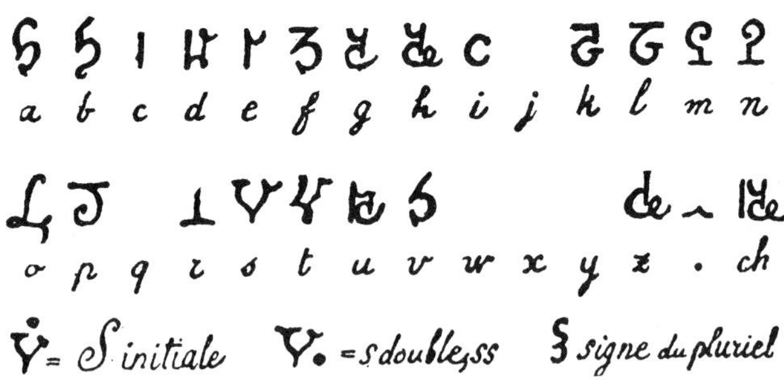

Hélène Smith's Martian alphabet

form; the Martian language was structured.

Neither her adventures on Mars, nor her incarnation as the Queen of France, lend much factual support for the theory of reincarnation. Both were remarkable performances, and undoubtedly quite convincing to the bulk of those who witnessed them. But the Marie Antoinette identification is too obvious. Who has not, at one time or another, believed that they were really a glamorous king or queen of another age? The Martian identification was too vague and uncheckable. In light of present knowledge it appears highly unlikely, to say the very least, that the planet Mars could contain the kind of life Hélène Smith described, indeed any sort of life at all, except possibly microscopic life. But when we come to the third of the dramas played out in Hélène Smith's séances, what Flournoy labeled the "Hindoo Cycle," there is a bit of puzzling evidence.

Hélène described herself as Simandini, the daughter of an Arab trader betrothed to an Indian prince. She received a declaration of love from the prince named Sivrouka Nayaka, in the palace of Tchandraguiri in the province of Kanara in the year 1401. She also described the palace as sort of an unfinished fortress. This appeared to be the sort of information that could be checked out. Flournoy dutifully inquired of several scholars of Indian history. They all replied that they never heard of Tchandraguiri, Kanara, or of a Prince Sivrouka Nayaka, and they doubted that such places or personage had ever existed. Flournoy was disappointed and annoyed, particularly since he himself was supposed to be a reincarnation of the prince, so he continued the search.

One day while browsing in a library he accidentally came across an old six-volume history of India by a man named De Marles. One volume contained the following passage:

"Kanara and the neighboring provinces on the side towards Delhi may be regarded as the Georgia of Hindustan; it is there, it is said, that the most beautiful women are to be found; the natives, however, are very jealous in guarding them, and do not often allow them to be seen by strangers.

"Tchandraguiri which signifies *Mountain of the Moon* is a vast fortress constructed, in 1401, by the rajah Sivrouka Nayaka. This prince, as also his successors, belonged to the sect of the Djains."

It was a wonderful moment and Flournoy was elated. He wrote, "At last! With what a beating heart did I fasten my eyes on that irrefutable historic evidence that my preceding incarnation, under the beautiful skies of India, was not a myth! I felt new life in my veins. I reread twenty times those blessed lines, and took a copy of them to send to those pretend savants who were ignorant even of the name of Sivrouka, and who allowed doubts to be cast upon his reality."

A wonderful moment, and a brief one. It turned out that the De Marles book, published in 1828, was regarded as untrustworthy in the late nineteenth century. Research in Indian history since that time has done nothing to enhance the author's reputation. Since De Marles rarely listed his sources it was impossible to know how he arrived at this particular story.

Though we don't know where De Marles got his information, we may make a pretty shrewd guess as to where Hélène Smith got hers—from the De Marles book. Copies were available in the Geneva library that she is known to have visited. She may have glanced at the book and this particular passage stuck in her remarkable memory, only to come back later during a séance. Naturally Hélène Smith would have no conscious recollection of this. To her it all seemed a very real part of a past life.

Mlle Smith's incarnation, Simandini, was originally supposed to have been the daughter of an Arab trader. At one point during a séance she was pressed to write something in her "native" tongue of Arabic. She did produce a short phrase in what appeared to be Arabic script. An apparent translation of the phrase is "The little from the friend [is] much."

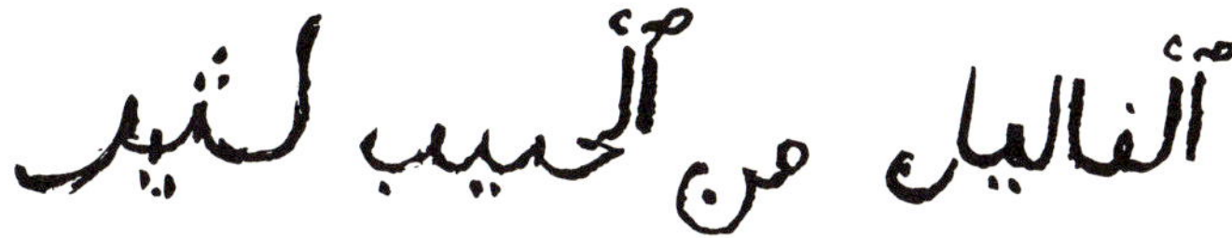

The fragment of Arabian script written by Mlle Smith. The translation reads, "the little from the friend [is] much."

Flournoy noted immediately that the medium had written the phrase from left to right, as one would write English or French. Arabic, however, is written from right to left. The characters were also drawn rather tentatively and painfully, more like someone was sketching a picture than writing in a language that they knew well. Flournoy suspected that this bit of Arabic was a phrase that Hélène Smith had seen at some point. Upon investigating he found that the text resembled a dedication which a Geneva physician had used several years previously in a book in the public library. Flournoy presumed that Hélène had looked into the book some six years before the trance episode, and the long-buried bit of Arabic script came to mind when she was pressed to write something in Arabic.

There is, of course, no way of proving Flournoy's suggestion, and the medium always denied that her Arabic was anything other than a genuine recollection of a past life. However, in view of the entire case, and of other known examples of Mlle Smith's remarkable memory, the suggestion seems more than a plausible one.

When Flournoy published his observations on Hélène Smith, she was deeply hurt and greatly outraged. Though his account is respectful, and sympathetic, he tried to explain all her visions, communications, and reincarnation in orthodox psychological terms, as products of her unconscious mind. He paid great tribute to the power and originality of Mlle Smith's unconscious imagination, and one cannot read his account without feeling a considerable degree of admiration for the medium. But Mlle Smith did not want explanations, no matter how respectful; she wanted confirmation. She would accept nothing less than uncritical praise of her powers. Her sense of betrayal must have been deeply felt, for she had already elevated Flournoy to the status of her prince-husband in her Indian incarnation. She cut off all communication with him, and refused to allow further scientific investigation of her condition, though one psychologist managed to keep track of her later career.

Hélène Smith's case attracted the attention of a wealthy American woman interested in spiritualism. She gave the medium an income which allowed her to quit her job and spend the rest of her life developing her psychic powers.

Freed from the necessity of earning a living in the real world, Hélène Smith would spend more and more time in her fantasy world. Perhaps her mental condition was deteriorating, and Professor Deonna, who studied her last years and published a book about her after her death in 1930, believed that by that time Hélène Smith's mental condition bordered on insanity. Perhaps the generosity of the American spiritualist was all that saved her from ending her life in a mental institution.

By the end of her life Hélène had come to regard herself as the reincarnation of Mary. She painted scenes from the New Testament under the guidance of the spirits that surrounded her. Her painting style was very odd. She would paint here and there all over the canvas, without any apparent purpose. Then, quite surprisingly, with the last few strokes she was able to tie all the parts together and make the picture complete.

The case of Hélène Smith may be extreme. Most people who genuinely believe that they can recall past lives, or that they are the reincarnation of this or that historical figure, do not display all of Hélène Smith's other strange symptoms. But it is also worth remembering that most have not been observed as closely over an extended period of time as had Mlle Smith. Generally such people associate only with believers, who neither require nor desire any additional evidence, and resolutely close their eyes to anything that might contradict their beliefs.

A person meeting Hélène Smith in the course of her work would never have guessed that this vigorous, hard-working woman was at night transported to Mars and India while entranced. There were no outward or obvious signs of mental abnormality. The possibility that she was a conscious fake does not even deserve serious consideration.

Her performance was an impressive one. She brought out information that should not have been available to her through "normal" means. All in all, if one had a tendency to believe in reincarnation, the case of Hélène Smith might support our belief, if we knew less about it. But Hélène Smith was too honest, too convinced of her powers, and Flournoy was too good an observer. All the imperfections were exposed to public view.

The lesson of Hélène Smith is a good one to keep in mind as we proceed through other "documented" cases of reincarnation.

6

Edgar Cayce's Life Readings

Undoubtedly one of the most influential figures in the current revival of interest in reincarnation is Edgar Cayce. It is hard to imagine how anyone living in America today could have failed to hear of Edgar Cayce. He has been the subject of countless books that have sold millions of copies.

Still, a little background will probably be helpful, for though a lot of people have heard something about Edgar Cayce being a "prophet" or a "psychic," they really don't know much else about him. Edgar Cayce was born in 1877 near Hopkinsville, Kentucky. His parents were poorly educated farmers and he received only an elementary education. Though Edgar was a deeply religious lad, and had wished to become a preacher, poverty forced him to give up the ambition and take a job as a salesman.

Then at the age of twenty-one Edgar Cayce quite mysteriously lost his voice, a serious enough affliction for anyone but deadly for a salesman. No orthodox treatment seemed to help. Finally Cayce was able to regain his voice temporarily when put into a trance by a traveling hypnotist. Later, under the guidance of a local man who had learned hypnotism, Cayce was shown how to put himself into a trance. While entranced he appeared able to diagnose and cure his own loss of voice. The amateur hypnotist was so impressed that he had Cayce diagnose and prescribe for a stomach condition that had troubled him for years. The treatment was apparently successful and Cayce was launched upon a career as a medical clairvoyant. He would lie down, go into a self-induced trance, and then diagnose the illness of persons who came to him seeking help. Soon he branched out into diagnosing persons who were not in the room. All he needed was an individual's name, and the date and place of his birth.

Cayce wasn't actually a healer, that is, he never claimed to possess any power to cure illness, but he usually did suggest a course of treatment. Cayce's treatments were always simple, consisting of changes in diet, certain exercises, and manipulation of the spine. The treatments were drawn from folk medicine, osteopathy, and other unorthodox medical practices. Many reported being cured after following Cayce's suggestions, and his reputation grew. By the time he died at the age of sixty-seven, he had a national reputation. He was known as "the Miracle Man of Virginia Beach." He had moved to that resort area in order to establish some sort of hospital, under the patronage of a wealthy admirer, but the venture collapsed during the depression, and Cayce himself was always dogged by financial difficulties.

During his own lifetime Cayce was known primarily as a medical clairvoyant. There have been many in American history. Cayce is just one of the most recent and most successful. But since his death Cayce's reputation has continued to grow. The Association for Research and Enlightenment that Cayce established is now run by his children. It is a virtual new religion, with Edgar Cayce as its prophet. He is unquestionably the most famous American psychic of the twentieth century. His fame no longer rests on his medical readings, but rather on a curious outgrowth of the medical readings.

While doing medical readings or "physical readings," as Cayce came to call them, he began to come up with some rather puzzling statements that he could not explain. For example, at the end of one of his readings he said of the subject, "He was once a monk." At the time it was claimed that Cayce had little interest in the idea of reincarnation, or in any of the broader religious and mystical questions that it posed. He was a Bible-believing Christian, and they never preached reincarnation in the church he went to. Indeed he seemed more than a little troubled that there was something wicked about fooling with the concept of reincarnation in the first place. But Edgar Cayce had gathered about himself friends and admirers who had no qualms at all about reincarnation. They encouraged him to embark upon a whole new area of psychic exploration that came to be known as "life readings."

Cayce would put himself into a trance and be given this sort of command:

"You will have before you (the person's name), born (his date of birth) in (his place of birth). You will give the relation of this entity and the universe, and the universal forces, giving the conditions which are as personalities, latent and exhibited, in the present life; also the former appearances on the earth plane, giving time, place, and the name; and that in each life which built or retarded the entity's development."

Once Cayce embarked on these "life readings" they became more detailed and frankly more bizarre. He talked about subjects' past lives in such places and times as the American South

Edgar Cayce

during the Civil War, France during the time of Louis XIV, ancient Rome, ancient Egypt, and finally on the lost continent of Atlantis.

Most historians, geologists, and other scholars believe that Atlantis never existed but Edgar Cayce talked a great deal about the previous incarnations of his subjects on Atlantis, and to hundreds of thousands and perhaps millions of Edgar Cayce enthusiasts today Atlantis seems as real as Rome and Egypt. In 1973 there was a well-financed, and well-publicized "psychic expedition" to find the "lost Atlantis." This expedition had been inspired in large measure by the pronouncements of Edgar Cayce. Despite optimistic predictions about great discoveries, the expedition found nothing of value, and soon faded from public view. It was significant only in that it was yet another example of the passionate devotion many people have to Edgar Cayce's ideas.

There is some disagreement among Cayce's numerous biographers as to when the psychic first developed an interest in reincarnation. According to one, it was not until 1923, when he was already in his mid-forties and well established in a career as a psychic. In this version the idea of reincarnation was first pressed on him by one of his subjects.

A recent biography, however, holds that Cayce's interest in the subject developed spontaneously at least a decade earlier. Cayce was giving a physical reading on a five-year-old child who was extremely nervous and high-strung. But instead of dealing immediately with the child's condition he started off on a new tack.

"With this entity, we have had a return from a previous experience frought with great fear. And with the entity, remembering this fear, special influences are now required into the experiences of this mind—so that it may be kept from fear, from loud and discordant noises, from darkness, the scream of shells in the night, the shouts of individuals, anything that caused the entity to experience fear in the past." Cayce's trance statements were usually couched in such vague and twisted language, making them difficult to understand and open to a variety of interpretations. In addition we cannot be sure how accurately they were transcribed.

But one thing quite clear about this reading was that Cayce was not talking about the child's present life, which had been quite peaceful, but about some past life. "And then the tramping of feet, the shouts of arms, the artillery shells bursting nearby brought destructive forces. The entity then was only two or three years older than in the present experience and now again, the rattling sabers, of those in this experience called the Night Riders, the burning of barns, the tramp of marching feet, the thunder of horses' hooves, the shouts in the night, all these awaken the old memories and fears."

What Cayce was saying was that the child's current nervous troubles had originated from some sort of war experience as a child in a previous lifetime. "This entity," said Cayce, "lived once in the country known as Poland, and was subject to the horrors of war and its devastation."

For treatment Cayce recommended that the boy be raised quietly, and kept away from disturbing influences as much as possible. "Then, as the child's personality unfolds, the entity will gradually become better adjusted until, alas, there will be another war in ten years or so of worldwide proportions."

That is yet another side to Edgar Cayce's alleged psychic abilities. Not only was he a medical clairvoyant, and an adept at reading an individual's past lives, he was also supposed to be a prophet of uncanny accuracy. Often while making a diagnosis he would slip in a prediction or two about the future. This one is taken by his followers to be an accurate prediction of the outbreak of World War I which did indeed begin about ten years from the time this particular reading was supposed to have been made.

Today many Cayce followers still search the carefully preserved transcripts of Cayce readings in an attempt to find clues to the future. As with most prophets, however, Cayce's statements require a great deal of interpretation. His prophecies can usually be related to events that have taken place up until the time the interpretation is being made. For the future, however, they have been poor guides. It is easy enough to look at the statement about another war, and count it as a prediction of World War I, because we already know when World War I began. But back in 1967 and 1968 a lot of people thought they had found in the readings of Edgar Cayce an equally clear prediction that there was going to be a major earthquake in California in 1968 or 1969. There was no major earthquake, and so the prophet's followers have revised their interpretations. They now contend Cayce said there will be a major earthquake in California sometime before the year 2000. This sort of prophetic waffling is highly suspect—and deservedly so.

But our interest here is in Edgar Cayce's readings on reincarnation, not his prophecies. After a couple of experiences like the one with the hysterical boy, Cayce decided to try a life reading on himself. He put himself into a trance, as usual, and his wife asked him about reincarnation. The entranced Cayce confirmed that the phenomenon was real and important.

Then she asked him, "In what way did the psychic knowledge of Edgar Cayce develop from the past?"

Cayce began speaking of an "entity" called Uhjltd. This Uhjltd—Cayce in a previous incarnation—was an Arabian prince. He was defeated in a battle against the Persians and left to die in the desert. He was badly wounded and suffering from hunger and thirst when he saw in the distance a desert oasis with three palm trees. Cayce had often dreamed of a desert oasis with three palm trees, but never had known what the dream was supposed to mean.

Cayce continued: "He tried pulling himself along by the arms, dragging his wounded legs, toward the well, suffering from hunger and thirst, as well as infection and loss of blood. As his strength waned, the realization came to him that only a superhuman effort of the will would ease his death throes."

And so, said Cayce, he withdrew into the "subconscious recesses" of his mind, hoping to die a quiet and painless death. But several hours later Uhjltd awakened to find that his wounds had healed and his fever had disappeared. He had the strength to get up and walk to the oasis to drink and quench his thirst. By this act, Cayce said, the entity that was later to emerge in the form of Edgar Cayce had developed his innate psychic forces to the point where they stayed within his "soul consciousness."

In other readings on himself Cayce revealed that he had once been a high priest in ancient Egypt, and in that incarnation too he had possessed great occult powers. He had also been a physician in ancient Persia, a foreshadowing of his twentieth-century interest in things medical.

Apparently Cayce first struggled against the concept of reincarnation, but after being shown the passages in the Bible which might conceivably point toward a belief in reincarnation, his doubts were resolved, and for the rest of his life he did not seem to worry overmuch about reincarnation as being non-Christian.

Cayce is said to have used the word "karma" in one of his trance utterances, before he ever became aware of the meaning of the word in his waking life. Certainly after he became a well-known psychic he must have heard a lot of discussion on the idea of karma from his friends and admirers, for the notion, as we have seen, has long been popular in psychic and occult circles.

Karma was what most appealed to Edgar Cayce about the idea of reincarnation. Many otherwise unexplainable illnesses could be traced to events in past lives. But most of all, karma implied that the universe was a place of order and justice, in which no one suffered without cause, and in which everyone had a chance for greater happiness or greater perfection in the next life, or the one after that.

A psychologist named Gina Cerminara became fascinated by Cayce, and in 1950 wrote a book based on his theories of reincarnation entitled *Many Mansions*. The book became a best-seller, and remains popular today after over twenty years. It was one of the early popular books about the theories of Edgar Cayce.

She described what the discovery of reincarnation and karma meant to Edgar Cayce:

"In those twenty-two years, a procession of suffering and bewildered humanity passed in review before the profound insight of Cayce's hypnotic clairvoyance. Physical and psychological ills of every description preoccupied these people; like the psalmist, who cried in uncomprehending anguish, they wanted to know *Why has this thing come upon me?*

"Not all cases were of desperate or tragic proportions—many

of the past life histories of these people were of no greater dramatic interest than the commonplace, ordinary lives they were leading in the present. But invariably, whether their problem was mild or severe, it was demonstrated that their situation of the present was a link in a chain of sequence that had begun centuries ago. In case after case, people were shown the cosmic relevance of their disease or their frustration. This knowledge had a transforming effect upon their lives; insight into the long-range pertinence of their situation enabled them to achieve dynamic equilibrium at higher levels of integration." In short, it made them feel better.

Cayce's emphasis on karma also explains much about his continuing popularity, and the religious devotion he inspires in his followers. Cayce's universe makes sense. No one suffers unjustly. If you are unhappy and unlucky in this lifetime, you are paying for the sins of a past life. If you bear your troubles well, return kindness for injustice, you will be repaid in a future life. One need not rage at the unfairness of life when an evil man appears to prosper. In some future life he will be brought down. Cayce said that in his own past lives he had been overproud, and sensual, and that is why he had been born into humble surroundings and been given a chance to use his psychic talents for the benefit of humanity.

Here is how karma worked out in a couple of typical Cayce readings. One concerns a beautiful New York model who made an unfortunate marriage. When her husband was sent overseas in World War II she began drinking heavily, sleeping with many men, and developed the habit of walking around nude while drunk. All the Cayce readings, by the way, exhibit an extremely puritanical streak, one typical of his early southern Christian upbringing. It appears that his journeys through other times, and other codes of morals, did not broaden his outlook. Indeed, one gets the distinct impression that, according to Cayce, the proper moral behavior for all times and all places is exactly the one that he was taught by his own parents.

The model's degradation, according to Cayce, began when she was a nun in a French convent at the time of Louis XIV. She had been stern and intolerant of human weakness. In this lifetime, her karma was, in a sense, paying her back by making her weak, and the object of the intolerant contempt of others.

In another and even more striking case a wealthy New York woman in her early fifties had suffered years of severe mental depression, for which no cause could be found, and for which no treatment was effective.

According to Cayce her problems arose from two previous lives. In one she had lived in Palestine at the time of Jesus. She was the wife of a Jewish priest, and very scornful of Jesus and his followers.

If that were not enough, she was reborn in Salem, Massachusetts, at the time of the witch trials. "The entity was among those who were very hard, very questioning, very condemning of those who had convincing evidence of the survival of personality. . . The entity then caused many hardships. When some were ducked, the entity was present and gave consent. When some were beaten with many stripes, the entity gave evidence and approval. Hence, in the present the entity finds itself bound with those periods when consciousness is hampered. There have been in the lacteal ducts and in the first and second cervicals lesions formed by pressures in the incoordination between the sympathetic and cerebro-spinal systems. This brings on periods of physical reaction."

So this proud and intolerant attitude expressed in two previous lives had brought on a karmic reaction of major proportions—enough indeed to absolutely ruin the present life. This appears just and makes sense, but there are problems, which are typical of Cayce readings.

First, the reading itself is rather vague. Cayce rarely gave proper names or exact dates in connection with past lives. In most cases this sort of information would have been of little use, since there would be little hope of locating evidence for the existence of a particular nun in a convent in the time of Louis XIV, still less for the wife of a Jewish priest in Palestine 2,000 years ago. However, in the case of the life in Salem at the time of the witch trials it is unfortunate the reading is so incomplete. The proceedings of the witch trials are very well documented and it would be possible to retrieve the name of anyone who, as the reading said, "gave evidence."

There are a couple of errors in the reading too. The witches at Salem were not whipped, nor were they ducked. Both techniques had been used to extract confessions from witches, but primarily in Europe, and not at all in Salem. But was Cayce really talking about the witch trials in the first place? He doesn't mention witches; that is merely an interpretation. He talks only about "those who had convincing evidence of the survival of personality." Surely that was not an issue in the witchcraft trials, for both accusers and accused believed in life after death.

There are problems even with the diagnosis. Cayce speaks rather generally, and in a rather confused manner, of problems centering in the spine. But the woman was suffering from severe depression, not a spinal disorder. Depression may have a physical cause, it may even have something to do with the spine, though this seems highly unlikely, but there is certainly no independent evidence that this woman was suffering from what Cayce said she was.

Karma, in the Edgar Cayce readings, can be extremely, even brutally, direct. A woman who suffered from numerous allergies was told how, in a previous lifetime, she had been a chemist and had produced many poisons which harmed others.

A man with stomach problems had been a glutton in the court of Louis XIII. Before that he had been a gluttonous physician in ancient Persia. Two lifetimes of overeating had brought about a third of indigestion.

The parents of an anemic child were told how five lifetimes back this particular child had been a ruler in Peru who had been responsible for the shedding of much blood, "hence anemia in the present."

Sometimes the retribution was more symbolic. A nobleman at the time of the French Revolution who had closed his ears to the pleas of the poor and suffering was reincarnated in the twentieth century as a deaf person.

Occasionally the karmic revenge even seems rather humorous. An entity who in early America had been responsible for ducking witches was born into a new life as a chronic bedwetter.

There is a large measure of free will included in the Cayce philosophy. If one is "good" in this life, then he can escape retribution in the next. The implications of such a doctrine could be quite radical but Cayce himself is profoundly conservative. Here is an example. Cayce knows that killing is wrong. Will a soldier suffer in future lives for killing enemies during a war? Not if he is doing his duty and acting under orders, says Cayce. A soldier will suffer retribution in a future life only if he "enjoys" the killing he is ordered to do. While Cayce seems to imply that we all bear an individual responsibility for our acts, that responsibility is also sharply limited by our station in life.

It is an easy and comfortable sort of philosophy to live with, and that is a great part of its appeal.

Edgar Cayce made over 2,500 life readings. But from the few examples cited so far you may have noticed that the same historical periods occur over and over again. Colonial America, ancient Persia, eighteenth-century France, ancient Egypt, and a few others. Given the huge number of historical times and places possible, the field of choice seems suspiciously narrow. Why didn't Cayce ever seem to do readings on people who had been Parthian warriors, Swiss lake dwellers, Olmecs, Etruscans, or Nubians? Critics say that this is because Cayce didn't know anything about the Parthians, Swiss lake dwellers, Olmecs, Etruscans, or Nubians, and even his convoluted style of speaking could not entirely hide his absolute lack of knowledge.

Cayce's supporters contend, however, that reincarnations tend to occur in fairly regular sequences. A common pattern is Atlantis, Egypt, Rome, the Crusades, and early Colonial America. Another was Atlantis, Egypt, Rome, France in the eighteenth century, and America during the Civil War.

In general, souls of one era tend to incarnate together in another era. Says Gina Cerminara, "This proceeds with orderly and rhythmic alternation, almost like the shifts of laborers in a factory."

In the universe envisioned by Edgar Cayce, people who know one another in this life probably knew one another in previous lives as well. People who were related in one age were very likely related in a past age. In his ramblings through his own past, Edgar Cayce found that he had been married to his own wife Gertrude, back in Egyptian times. Then she was an exotic temple dancer, quite a change from the rather plain-looking twentieth-century version. But then it is a little difficult to cast "American as apple pie" Edgar Cayce as the Arabian prince Uhjltd, or the Egyptian high priest Ra-Ta.

Now it is really quite charming to envision oneself meeting friends and relations in different times under different guises, almost like a cosmic costume party, in which half the fun is sorting out who is impersonating whom.

The justice of Cayce's karma is extraordinarily attractive. It dramatically confirms the Biblical injunction "as ye sow, so shall ye reap," if not in this lifetime then in another.

Despite all the suffering one might undergo in this lifetime or another, the Cayce philosophy is tremendously optimistic. Though there seems to be no entirely clear or consistent philosophy about how one is reborn, Cayce's ideas appear to include a measure of free will, that is, the entity is allowed, up to a point, to pick the circumstances of its next birth in order to work off some karmic debt or develop some sort of innate power. There is implied in all of this the idea that the whole of mankind, all of those souls or entities, is striving toward some sort of ultimate perfection.

This is all very nice, very optimistic, and very satisfying, but is it true? Accepting Edgar Cayce's life readings as a proof of reincarnation presents a number of formidable difficulties.

Most Christians are not as easily satisfied, as was Edgar Cayce, by a few ambiguous Bible references as proof that the theory of reincarnation is in accord with the teaching of Jesus.

Even Cayce's most devoted followers admit that hard, tangible proof of reincarnation is difficult to come by through the Cayce readings. The statements about past lives are too vague and uncheckable. As we have pointed out, they often contain statements which are historically inaccurate. The response to such inaccuracies by Cayce followers is twofold. First, that this sort of psychic material is not always precise, and that it is the general thrust of the material rather than the details that are important. Second, Cayce followers say that the historians may be wrong. Historians, after all, are depending upon secondhand information, whereas the entities whose lives are being related by Edgar Cayce were actually there, and must be regarded as the best witnesses. Primarily, though, the Cayce followers insist that the readings "make sense" and there is no other logical way of explaining why certain things happen to people.

Another common defense of Cayce's life readings is saying that since so many of his other psychic feats have been "proved," his statements about reincarnation, which are far more difficult to check out, must also be true, though no hard evidence is available. But how good is the evidence for Cayce's other psychic feats, primarily clairvoyant diagnosis and prophecy?

A story retold in practically all Cayce biographies is how Hugo Munsterberg, a professor of psychology from Harvard, came to visit Cayce in Virginia Beach and went away very impressed. The story sounds good to anyone who knows the history of psychical research, for Munsterberg was a fierce and persistent foe of fraudulent spirit mediums and had exposed some of the more famous ones. His testimony in favor of Cayce would have been worth listening to. But here is the problem—we don't have his testimony. Cayce biographers like to invent conversations in which the crusty professor is baffled by the country psychic. However, we have no firsthand statement from Munsterberg himself. There is more evidence, admittedly circumstantial, that Munsterberg was unimpressed. At the time, the American Psychic Society, of which Munsterberg was a member, was considering a study of Cayce but abandoned the idea after Munsterberg met him. It is more reasonable to assume that if Munsterberg had really been impressed by Cayce the organization would have undertaken the study. In all fairness Munsterberg cannot be called as a witness against Cayce, but he can't be called as a witness for the defense either.

Cayce supporters point to "thousands of documented cases of proven correct diagnosis and cure." But this material substantially adds up to transcribed notes of Cayce readings, and letters of gratitude from individuals who felt that Cayce had helped them. Such testimonials sound good, but are a long, long way from adequate medical records. Every snake-oil dealer, patent medicine man, in short, every quack healer in the world, has a flock of similar testimonials to the great value of his wares. Many of the testimonials are doubtless sincere, but trying to determine whether a course of treatment is effective or not is an extraordinarily difficult task.

Harry Edwards, a British spiritual healer, has lived longer and been much more active than Edgar Cayce was. He has many times the number of testimonials to his powers as does Cayce. Yet his view of the universe is entirely different from Cayce's. Medical authorities in Britain concede that Edwards is probably sincere, but insist that his records, which are better than Cayce's, prove nothing whatever. There has never been a successful investigation of the claims of any medical clairvoyant or faith healer, Edgar Cayce included.

How about the Cayce predictions? If he can predict the future, then we should at least seriously consider the possibility that he can also read the past. But can he predict the future? We have already mentioned his apparent prediction of a great earthquake in California in 1968 or 1969, an earthquake that failed to occur. Back in 1943, Cayce predicted that within the next twenty-five years China would move toward Christianity and democracy. Some of Cayce's followers try to "prove" that he is really correct by saying there is a great Christian underground in China, but there's no saving the prophecy; it is simply wrong.

Sometimes Cayce followers seem to invent evidence to prove their hero correct. Cayce had more or less predicted that the lost continent of Atlantis would begin rising off Bermuda, of all places, in about 1968. The California earthquake was to be part of the worldwide cataclysms that there to accompany the rising of Atlantis. For several years Cayce followers kept saying that Atlantis was coming up. There were many articles and even a couple of books to that effect. Photographs of underwater rock formations were labeled as photos of "ancient walls" emerging from the sea bottom. In fact, there was no lost continent rising off Bermuda or anywhere else. Recently Cayce followers have been rather quiet about the lost continent which by their timetable should now be fully visible. But they have not admitted they are wrong either.

Did Edgar Cayce have *any* correct predictions? That depends upon just how strict one's criteria are. Cayce was supposed to have predicted the stock market crash of 1929. What he really said was, "Better than a few points were missed here and there, even in a spectacular rise or fall than to be worrying where the end would be. Forget not the warning here." Not exactly an unambiguous prediction, is it?

There are so many Cayce predictions, and they are so vaguely stated, that it is possible to find one that can be applied to practically any situation, particularly if one is not too demanding.

So one cannot prove reincarnation by Edgar Cayce's life readings. Nor is there any solid evidence that Cayce possessed "psychic" abilities of any sort.

The enormous popularity of Edgar Cayce is not due to the proof of his powers, but rather to the vision of life that he presented. His universe is just and hopeful. There is no suffering without cause, no goodness without reward. It is by far a better universe than the cold and indifferent one outlined by science. And so it appeals to a sense of "inner reality" in many people. It just seems to make more sense, and because it does, things like tangible evidence become largely superfluous, mere frosting on the cake, for those who already believe.

This attitude is well expressed by Gina Cerminara in the conclusion of her book, *Many Mansions*:

"There are many people of the Western world who cannot accept the world view of the Eastern religions, the view reaffirmed by the Cayce readings. And yet, though they cannot accept it without more rigorous scientific evidence than that provided by the Cayce data, they may find it difficult to deny that the reincarnationist view is precise, rational, and intelligible; that it is psychologically credible, ethically sound, and scientifically plausible. To the person who can accept it, reincarnation offers a purpose for living, a pole-star by which to travel, and an assurance that he is not lost in a meaningless chaos of forces over which he has no ultimate control."

It is almost saying that if reincarnation isn't true it should be.

7

The Strange Case of Bridey Murphy

Practically everyone who lived in America during the 1950s will be familiar with the name, Bridey Murphy. The name was supposed to be that of an early nineteenth-century Irish woman, who had been reincarnated as a mid-twentieth-century American housewife.

No single tale of reincarnation has attracted such widespread attention during this century. A book called *The Search for Bridey Murphy* became a huge bestseller. All over the country people who had never heard of reincarnation before started talking about it. A lot of people began "discovering former lives," by "age regression" through hypnosis.

Bridey Murphy also became a fad. No comedian could get through a routine without some Bridey Murphy joke. Costume parties were called "Bridey Murphy balls" and people held "come-as-you-were" parties.

But it wasn't all fun and games. The Bridey Murphy case stirred up an astonishing amount of opposition and real hostility. Scientists, physicians, psychiatrists, historians, and ministers were outraged. They launched a noisy and, in the end, very successful attack against the Bridey Murphy reincarnation story.

It was so successful that if you didn't live through the Bridey Murphy craze, you may have never heard the name. The case is still cited by hard-core believers in reincarnation, but the general public has largely forgotten. Yet the whole Bridey Murphy incident presents a fascinating look at the sort of evidence that is often presented as proof of reincarnation, and of public attitudes toward the subject.

The case began in 1952 with a Pueblo, Colorado, businessman named Morey Bernstein. For some years Bernstein had been interested in the subject of hypnosis. He had read a great deal about it, attended lectures and demonstrations, and ultimately became a practiced and knowledgeable amateur hypnotist, and had often demonstrated his skills on friends and acquaintances.

Bernstein was also familiar with Edgar Cayce's life readings, and was strongly inclined to believe in reincarnation. He knew that a common technique for psychiatrists who use hypnosis was "age regression," that is, taking the hypnotized subject farther and farther back into his or her own early life in order to bring up memories of childhood that might be forgotten or suppressed. But Bernstein had heard that it was also possible to put hypnotized subjects through an age regression that would allow them to recall events in previous lives. He was eager to try such an experiment.

For his subject he chose a woman he called "Ruth Simmons." Ruth Simmons was a pseudonym for Virginia Tighe, a resident of Pueblo, Colorado, and a casual acquaintance of Bernstein. Bernstein chose Mrs. Tighe because on a previous occasion she had shown herself to be an excellent hypnotic subject, and

Morey Bernstein, author of The Search for Bridey Murphy

because he felt that she had little previous knowledge of, or interest in, reincarnation.

The sessions started on Saturday, November 29, 1952. Bernstein had his tape recorder running through each session. First, he took the subject on a normal age regression back to the age of one. Then he said:

"Be looking at yourself when you were one year old. Now go back, even farther back. Oddly enough, you can go even farther back.

"I want you to keep on going back and back and back in your mind. And surprising as it may seem, strange as it may seem, you will find that there are other scenes in your memory. There are other scenes from faraway lands and distant places in your memory . . ."

When the subject spoke again her voice sounded strange, unlike that of Virginia Tighe. She talked about having scratched the paint off of her metal bed, and when she was asked her name she said:

". . . Uh . . . Friday."

"Your name is what?"

"Friday."

"Don't you have any other name?"

"Uh . . . Friday Murphy."

"And where do you live?"

". . . I live in Cork . . . Cork."

Later the name was determined to be Bridey Murphy. Cork is a city in Ireland, and she said that she was eight years old, and that the year was 1806.

Bernstein and his subject had a total of six hypnotic sessions between November 29, 1952, and August 29, 1953. The outlines of the past life that emerged were this: Bridey (Bridget) Kathleen Murphy was an Irish girl born in Cork in 1798. She was the daughter of a Protestant barrister (lawyer) in Cork named Duncan Murphy, and his wife Kathleen. She had two brothers. One died while she was still a baby, the other grew up to marry the daughter of the mistress of a school they had both attended.

At the age of twenty Bridey married Sean Brian Joseph McCarthy, also the child of a Cork barrister, but a Catholic. The couple moved to Belfast, where Sean eventually taught law at the Queen's University. They had no children, and Bridey died at the age of sixty-six, and was buried in Belfast in 1864.

During the hypnotic sessions the subject also mentioned an even earlier life in New Amsterdam, now New York, in Colonial America. But in this incarnation she had died while still a baby, and could provide no details about life at that time. Besides, the memories of this life seemed painful, so Bernstein dropped the pursuit. In fact, even as Bridey Murphy, the subject failed to provide an overwhelming number of hard details about her life.

When asked the distance between Cork and Belfast, the two places in which she was supposed to have lived, Bridey Murphy replied:

"Uh . . . uh . . . it's in a different province. Uh . . . Belfast is . . . no . . . Belfast is . . . uh-uh . . . in a different province . . . I don't know how far away it is."

She was unable to name any mountain in Ireland, and appeared completely ignorant of the elements of the Catholic Mass, though she had married a Catholic and lived in a deeply Catholic country.

Some of the information she provided was apparently dead wrong. For example, she mentioned a lake which doesn't seem to have ever existed.

A lot of what she said was fairly obvious. When first asked

for examples of Irish words, she came up with things like *colleen* and *banshee*, words that practically anyone would have known. She also talked about the Blarney Stone, another bit of "Irish lore" familiar to almost everyone today. Here she even appears to have incorrectly described how one reaches the stone. Worse still, the tradition of kissing the Blarney Stone may not even have been established at the time Bridey was supposed to have lived.

On the other hand, she did appear to know things about Ireland in the eighteenth century that would or should have been unknown to an American housewife of the mid-twentieth century. She knew about Queen's University in Belfast, a placed called The Meadows in Cork, and about the legend of Deirdre, a popular Irish myth, but one not well known in the United States. The use of words like "barrister" instead of "lawyer," implied that the speaker was from the British Isles rather than America.

There was nothing utterly unique or sensational about the Bridey Murphy case up to this point. People interested in the subject of reincarnation could cite dozens of similar cases. Any popular book on reincarnation will contain accounts of far more interesting and exciting past lives than the one attributed to this rather dull nineteenth-century Irish woman.

But Bridey had a stroke of luck, for the story came to the attention of William J. Barker, a feature writer for the Denver *Post's* Sunday magazine *Empire*. Barker was intrigued, though a bit skeptical at first. A meeting with Bernstein impressed him. Morey Bernstein was a very solid citizen indeed. He had a successful business and plenty of money and therefore no reason to pull off any sort of money-making hoax. He had not actively sought out publicity, and was at first a bit leery of it. Moreover, he was an open and outgoing sort of person who just exuded sincerity. Barker decided that he was dealing with an honest man.

Then he listened to tapes of the Bridey Murphy hypnotic sessions and concluded, "Either I was hearing the voice of a consummate actress under the guidance of an adept director who'd written a masterly script—or this was truly spontaneous—genuinely what it sounded to be—evidence of a fantastic memory released through hypnosis."

Bernstein then hypnotized Barker's wife Lydia and she began to recount scenes that sounded like they came out of the American Revolutionary War. That convinced Barker, and apparently his editors as well, and he was given the go-ahead to do a series of features on Bridey Murphy. These appeared in *Empire* magazine on September 12, 19, and 26, 1954.

The response to the series was good, so good in fact that it inspired Bernstein to write his own account. His *The Search for Bridey Murphy*, which appeared in January, 1956, was nationally syndicated in newspapers, and in shortened form appeared in a popular national magazine. Quite suddenly the whole country went slightly Bridey Murphy crazy.

I remember attending parties where half the people were trying to hypnotize the other half and "regress" them into past lives. It seemed that almost everyone had a story concerning someone who, under hypnosis, had recalled life in the Old West or Cleopatra's Egypt, or some other suitably exotic time and place. I was hypnotized myself, though I was never able to "regress" much beyond the age of six, nor did I ever personally witness anything that might remotely have been called a successful age regression.

The Bridey Murphy phenomenon had about it all the massive silliness of other popular fads. It was foolish, but harmless enough, and yet quite soon there developed a distinctly nasty reaction. It turned out that there were a lot of people in America who really got angry over the idea of reincarnation. More time and effort was given to investigating and ultimately debunking *The Search for Bridey Murphy* than is usually accorded to books of this type.

There was a flood of angry denunciations from psychiatrists who disliked what they considered Bernstein's rather cavalier use of hypnosis. Hypnosis has a rather shady past, and the field had long been dominated by entertainers, charlatans, and cranks. Psychiatrists and other medical people felt that they had gone a long way toward rescuing the practice from the sins committed in its name, and transforming it into a valuable and respectable therapeutic tool. They actively discouraged parlor hypnosis. Then along came Bernstein and Bridey, to put the whole thing back on what they considered a carnival footing.

Historians were equally outraged by what they believed were the massive errors in Bridey's description of life in nineteenth-century Ireland. The clergymen were perhaps the angriest of all, for they felt that reincarnation was unscriptural, un-Christian, and presented a potential danger to religion.

By far the most damaging attack on the Bridey story was made in a series of articles printed in May and June of 1956 in the Hearst newspaper, the Chicago *American*, and later syndicated in other Hearst papers. The source of the attack is interesting, for Hearst papers had regularly printed enthusiastic articles about psychic phenomena in the past. The findings of the Chicago *American* articles were summarized and amplified in a brief article in *Life* magazine, at the time the most widely read and influential magazine in the country.

What the Chicago *American* reporters had done was investigate Virginia Tighe's early life. She had been born in Wisconsin in 1923, and at the age of three had been adopted by an aunt in Chicago where she lived until she was twenty. The reporters found what they believed to be a remarkable number of parallels between Bridey's life and Virginia's. The conclusion was that practically everything Bridey said could be traced to something in Virginia's early life.

The Denver *Post*, which by that time had developed an emotional stake in Briday Murphy, responded with a series of articles charging that the Chicago *American* articles were unproven and unfair. They also printed a long interview with Virginia Tighe, who also charged that the Chicago *American* articles about her childhood were incorrect.

Barker went to Ireland to try to find traces of the real historical Bridey, and his findings were published as an appendix in the paperback edition of *The Search for Bridey Murphy.*

The controversy raged on, but in the end the skeptics prevailed in the publicity battle. People first doubted Bridey, and then forgot her. Symbolic of Bridey's fall from prominence is the fact that at the height of the Bridey craze a movie called *The Search for Bridey Murphy* was started. Producers originally had high hopes for the film, but between production and release the Bridey bubble had collapsed. I have met only one person who ever saw the film, and he was the magazine editor who bought the first syndication rights of the Bridey story. He saw the film at a preview, and could not even recall whether it had been released to the public, so deep was the obscurity into which the name Bridey Murphy had sunk.

Noel Langley, who wrote and directed the Bridey Murphy film, thought there had been a conspiracy against it from the beginning.

"In the screenplay, I was limited to the material Bernstein had published in his book, though there was far more dramatic and convincing material elsewhere on the original tapes. The climax of the picture was carefully constructed to scare the public off the irresponsible use of hypnosis as a party-trick, and I even wrote in a gratuitous scene where a Protestant minister and a Catholic priest gave their definitive opinions on the theory of reincarnation (subversive paganism), and hypnosis (for the birds)."

Still, says Langley, there were all kinds of troubles in the studio. It got so bad that he nicknamed the unit in which the film was being shot the "Contamination Ward." "My production manager had been privately informed that the picture would never be finished, but that Duggan [the producer] and I already were."

Langley never quite says why the picture was sabotaged, though he implies some sort of antireincarnation plot. It seems more reasonable to assume that the studio thought they had a loser and were trying to get rid of it. In any case the picture was finished, though Langley says he never had a chance to cut it properly. It was released, but so quietly that few ever saw it. "When it was released, the general press gave it the silent treatment and it obediently wilted on the vine."

It may be significant that a decade later Alan J. Lerner's musical *On a Clear Day You Can See Forever*, which also dealt with reincarnation, enjoyed considerable success, and aroused no hostility. But of course, that story was not supposed to be true; Bridey Murphy was.

Today, however, nearly twenty years after the original Bridey boom, there appears to be a modest Bridey Murphy revival going on. As already mentioned, a segment of the hard-core believers in reincarnation never abandoned the Irish lass at all. They have spent years taking potshots at Bridey's debunkers, and have by this time pretty well convinced themselves that her critics were unfair, biased, and often dishonest. The Bridey Murphy case still remains a classic reincarnation story, and so even at this late date it is worth taking a closer look at the evidence for and against.

It is impossible to review the whole complicated, and usually angry, Bridey Murphy controversy here. But we will look at a few of the major points of contention.

As we noted, the most damaging charge brought against the Bridey story was that much of what Bridey recalled about life in Ireland in the nineteenth century was supposed to have been explainable by Virginia Tighe's own early experiences.

The Chicago *American* series said that Mrs. Tighe had an Irish aunt, who had "regaled" her with stories about Ireland when she was young. Mrs. Tighe, however, remembers the events quite differently. The aunt, Mrs. Marie Burns, was of Scotch-Irish descent and born in New York. Mrs. Tighe says she never knew her aunt very well and had not been regaled with Irish stories or anything else.

Under hypnosis Bridey had spoken of an "Uncle Plezz." The Chicago reporters found someone named Plezz, who claimed to have known Virginia when she was living in Chicago. The report however declined to give the full name and address of "Uncle Plezz." Virginia Tighe says that she remembers no such person, in this life at any rate.

The climax of the Chicago *American* series, however, was the revelation that while Virginia was growing up in Chicago, she had lived across the street from a woman named Corkell. This woman's premarriage name had been Murphy—Bridie (with an ie, not a y) Murphy. A really weird coincidence, or something, was that this Mrs. Bridie Murphy Corkell happened to be the mother of the editor of the Sunday edition of the Chicago *American* at the time the articles were published.

Virginia did not deny ever knowing the Corkell family, in fact, she remembered a "Buddy Corkell" fairly well and recalled being in the Corkell house several times. But she did deny ever knowing that Mrs. Corkell's name was Bridie Murphy. She did not remember ever speaking to Mrs. Corkell at all. She said she had not even known that Mrs. Corkell's first name was Bridie.

The second major area of controversy involves evidence for the existence of Bridey in Ireland. Though Barker and others have gone to Ireland they have found no verification that a barrister named Duncan Murphy and his wife Kathleen lived in Cork in 1798 and had a daughter, Bridget Kathleen; nor that a Bridget Kathleen Murphy married a Catholic named Sean Brian Joseph McCarthy, nor that she died in 1864. Indeed there is no evidence that any of the persons mentioned by Bridey ever existed, and there is not even evidence that St. Theresa's church, in which Bridey and Sean were supposed to have had their Catholic marriage, ever existed.

Records of births, marriages, deaths, and so forth in nineteenth-century Ireland are not all that complete. Traces of a poor family with few children might well have disappeared, but Bridey claimed to be the daughter of a barrister, married to the son of a barrister who later became a teacher of law at a prominent university. Some trace of such solidly middle-class people should certainly have turned up, and yet there is nothing.

The lack of evidence is damaging, but is it reasonable to

expect that the Bridey personality told the whole and correct story of her life? Bernstein has written, "I think it only reasonable to expect that some of Bridey's memoirs are colored, that some are in error, and that even key dates might be in error. But this is not an area from which an airtight case should be expected. The whole issue, rather, is whether the principles involved here merit more intensive consideration."

After Barker failed to find any evidence for the existence of Bridey, he speculated that perhaps she had been upgrading her family status. Bridey's answers under hypnosis were not always clear and consistent. At one point she seemed to be indicating that her father was really a farmer, not a barrister. Barker guesses that perhaps he was a farmer who did a bit of bookkeeping or other work for a barrister. He suggests that Bridey may never have been entirely clear about what her father did. She would, however, have been clear about what her husband did, and there is no trace of him either, although there should have been.

There are two conclusions one can draw from the evidence or lack of it. One that Bridey did exist, or may have existed, but was lying about her social status. Second, Bridey never existed, and there is no trace of a Bridey Murphy because there was never one.

Bridey did appear to be correct on some minor, but possibly significant, points. She mentioned two Belfast grocers from whom she bought "foodstuffs." They were Farr's and John Carrigan. Grocers with those names apparently did live in Belfast at about the time of Bridey's death. She also talked about a big rope company and a tobacco house in Belfast; both did exist.

In many other cases, however, there was no trace of places that she mentioned. This does not mean that they didn't exist but simply that there is no record of them, or that Bridey had misnamed them.

Some of the difficulties involved in trying to confirm, or dispute, the statements of Bridey Murphy can be seen in the very first statement she made, when she emerged during Bernstein's hypnosis. She talked about being punished for having scratched her "metal bed." Critics first asserted that there were no metal beds in Ireland when Bridey was supposed to have scratched hers. That would have been about 1802, for Bridey was very young at the time. Iron beds were not supposed to have been introduced in Ireland until after 1850. But Bridey's defenders have found evidence that iron bedsteads were being advertised for sale in Ireland as early as 1830, and perhaps earlier. Besides, she didn't say iron bed, she said metal bed, and perhaps her bed was brass. Brass beds apparently did exist in Ireland in 1802, though they were far from common.

But did Bridey really say metal bed in the first place? The quality of the tape recordings of the sessions is not first-rate. Taping equipment was not as sophisticated in 1952 as it is today, and much of what Bridey said is mumbled or otherwise unclear. Even today there can be a great deal of controversy over the interpretation of what is heard on a tape. On rehearing the tape some have concluded that Bridey was talking about scratching her "little" bed. There may or may not have been metal beds in Ireland in 1802, but as a child of four Bridey certainly had a "little" bed.

Another problem of interpretation comes when Bridey describes having grown up in a "wood house." Wood was scarce in Ireland at the time and most of the houses were stone, so a wood house is unlikely though not impossible. Yet on a rehearing of the tape some believe that Bridey said a "good" house, that is, a nice house.

And this problem becomes even more complicated when Bridey gets down to proper names or Irish words. As often as not it is impossible to decide with any precision what she said, and one interprets the statement according to whether one is pro- or anti-Bridey.

Perhaps the best single bit of evidence for the existence of a Bridey Murphy in Ireland in the nineteenth century comes from her mention of having lived in the "meadows" in Cork when a child. As it turned out there was a place in Cork called Mardike Meadows in 1801. A map showing Mardike Meadows appears as the end papers for the revised edition of *The Search for Bridey Murphy*. The name did not exist in the twentieth century, and it is highly unlikely that any modern Irish man or woman would have known of it, and therefore virtually impossible that Virginia Tighe could have run across the information in this life.

But as always, the evidence turns out to be less than conclusive. Bridey didn't say she lived in or near Mardike Meadows, but simply "the meadows," and that is a fairly common name; there are lots of places called "the meadows." The Chicago *American* reporters found that when Virginia Tighe was growing up she lived near some meadows. Virginia didn't recall the place ever being called "the meadows," but there is also no indication that the people of Cork called Mardike Meadows "the meadows" either. People may have called it Mardike, or something else entirely.

There are many, many other points of controversy, but the

ones mentioned so far should give you a pretty good idea of the nature of the argument. The attitude one has toward the controversy depends largely upon how you look at the problem.

Defenders of Bridey Murphy say that the critics have not proved that Bridey Murphy did not exist in nineteenth-century Ireland, nor have they shown conclusively that all of the things about Ireland that came out in Virginia Tighe's hypnotic sessions as Bridey were traceable to her early life in Wisconsin and Chicago. Certainly the case against Bridey is far from complete. Critics have made serious errors. One asserted that Virginia, like Bridey, had a brother who died at birth. That was false. But it is also notoriously difficult to prove a negative.

Much of the criticism of the Chicago *American*'s reconstruction of Virginia Tighe's early life is based on Mrs. Tighe's statements that she didn't remember the events or individuals, or that she remembered them differently. Certainly she is the best witness for her own childhood, but can her testimony be entirely believed? She was, by that time, pretty well committed to the Bridey Murphy idea. To admit that it all originated in some stray incidents in her own life would have been to look rather foolish, or worse.

Besides, she may really not have remembered any of that information consciously. Forgotten memories are often retrieved under hypnosis, though they may come out in a garbled fashion. One of the primary uses of hypnosis in psychotherapy is to get people to recall things that have been erased from their conscious minds. So it is quite possible that Virginia Tighe was telling the absolute truth about not remembering the name of her neighbor as being Bridie Murphy, and yet such incidents may still have been stuck in her unconscious mind, only to be released under Morey Bernstein's hypnosis.

But why would she have chosen this rather bizarre way of relating her own early experiences? She could have been instructed to do so by hypnotist Bernstein. But there has been no serious suggestion that conscious fraud played any part in the Bridey Murphy case. Most of those who met Bernstein, even if they were skeptical of reincarnation, were convinced that at least he was honest, and really believed that he had gotten in touch with the reincarnated personality of a woman who had been dead for a hundred years. But prior to the Bridey Murphy investigation Bernstein had already been a firm believer in reincarnation, and he set out to prove his beliefs when he took Virginia Tighe on her "age regression."

Hypnotic subjects are exceptionally responsive to the commands of the hypnotist. Indeed, it has been proposed that the hypnotic "state" or "trance" is nothing more than a condition of heightened suggestibility. The hypnotist does not have complete control over his subject, but the subject does try to be as agreeable as possible. I can recall that when I was hypnotized and sent on an "age regression" I was asked to make a drawing as I would have before I had taken art lessons. I began art lessons when I was about seven or eight, so I made a drawing of a human figure as a six-year-old would have made one. I don't know whether the drawing I made under hypnosis really resembled drawings that I had made when I was six, or whether I was simply making the sort of drawing that I imagined a six-year-old would make. Had I really been brought back to the age of six and was drawing as a six-year-old, or was I imitating the drawings of a six-year-old because I had been told to do so? I'm not sure.

Similarly one cannot be sure whether Virginia Tighe was really speaking as Bridey Murphy, or had simply made up the character (though unconsciously) from fragments of her youth to carry out the hypnotist's suggestion.

The critic's view of the problem is different from that of the supporter. The critic asks for conclusive evidence that a Bridey Murphy did exist, and that, while speaking as Bridey Murphy, Virginia Tighe produced information about nineteenth-century Ireland that she could not have known through normal means, or simply by a lucky shot.

Even Bridey's most ardent supporters admit that some of the things she said are clearly wrong. For example, she uses the word "Britisher" to describe an Englishman. But Britisher is an Americanism, and a word that no resident of Ireland in the nineteenth, or even twentieth, century is likely to have used. How did it, and other errors, appear in Bridey's conversation? According to Barker: "Bridey, taken at face value, is Ruth Simmons [the pseudonym for Virginia Tighe] remembering who she used to be. But Ruth Simmons never ceases entirely to be her present American self just because her fantastic recollection is being put into words. She employs many Americanisms in narrating the life of Bridey—her hair is 'real' red, she ate 'candy,' and so on."

Bridey's defenders say her story must be proved false, while her critics say it must be proved true. One side hasn't proved anything to the other side's satisfaction.

And if you think the problem is difficult for the person who wishes to decide simply whether Bridey Murphy is a case of reincarnation or unconscious fraud, imagine the difficulties faced by those who believe in spirit communication, clairvoyance, retrocognition, and a whole host of other paranormal or psychic phenomena. C. J. Ducasse is a Professor Emeritus of Philosophy from Brown University, and a man who a long-standing interest in various psychic phenomena. He reviewed the Bridey Murphy case in the *Journal of the American Society for Psychical Research* in 1962, after the excitement had died down. He spends page after page roasting Bridey's critics, pointing out their errors, and shortcomings. He painstakingly shows how many of Bridey's statements are or could have been true, and one assumes that he is going to wind up with a resounding cheer for the theory of reincarnation. Not so. He ends his article with this rather puzzling paragraph:

"On the other hand, for reasons other than those which were advanced by those various hostile critics, but which there is no space here to develop, the verifications summarized by Barker, of obscure points in Ireland mentioned in Bridey's six recorded conversations with Bernstein, do not prove that Virginia is a reincarnation of Bridey, nor do they establish a particularly strong case for it. They do, on the other hand constitute fairly strong evidence that in the hypnotic trances, paranormal knowledge of one or another kinds concerning these recondite facts of nineteenth-century Ireland became manifest."

So there is yet a third opinion, and a very common one in certain circles. Even those psychical researchers with a strong interest in reincarnation have strong doubts about the case of Bridey Murphy.

It is unlikely at this late date that any significant new information about Bridey Murphy is going to turn up. So nothing is going to be solved. The case of Bridey Murphy will continue to hang there like a mirror; everyone who looks into it will see confirmation of his own theories reflected back at him.

8

The Scientific Evidence

For nearly a century psychical researchers have been trying to find scientific proof that the soul, or the spirit, or the human personality (you may call it what you will) survives bodily death.

During most periods of history, and for the majority of people today, the survival of the soul after death is not a proposition in need of scientific proof. Some idea about survival after death is basic to most religions. Religious people need no more scientific proof of survival than they need scientific proof of the existence of God.

But about a century ago a sharp conflict between religion and science began to develop, particularly in England and the United States. Many well-educated people were both religious and very respectful of science. They believed that, given enough time, science would provide a firm empirical basis for traditional religious beliefs. But slowly science began to reveal a universe which was not at all like the one they had pictured on the basis of their early religious training.

Charles Darwin's theory of evolution, first proposed in 1859, was a particularly difficult development to take into account. If the human race had evolved from lower animals, and was not a product of special creation, then the concept of the human soul as something unique and immortal was brought into serious question. Without the soul, the whole idea of survival after death and a cosmic system of rewards and punishments simply melted away. Such developments were highly disturbing.

Still, the scientific method of investigation could not be abandoned simply because one did not like the results that the investigators were coming up with. A small but active number of scholars retained the hope that science could be used to prove the survival of the personality after death, if only the search were conducted in the right places and with the right attitude. It was out of this point of view that psychical research, and ultimately the scientific discipline known as parapsychology, grew.

Psychical research first began investigating the claims of spiritualist mediums. Here were individuals said to be reporting messages from the spirits of the dead. If these messages were authentic communications from beyond the grave, then the case for survival was spectacularly proved. At first it seemed as though all that was needed was for the mediums to deliver some information that could not have been known to them, but known only to the dead person.

That wasn't as easy as it sounds. As we have seen in the case of Hélène Smith, mediums were very difficult to deal with, and their communications from the world of the spirits were often confused, vague, and uncheckable. Hélène Smith, though she may have been mad, was one of the better mediums. Many a respectable researcher staked his reputation on the authenticity of a spirit medium who turned out to be a shoddy fraud.

Psychical researchers ran into another problem. Even if the

medium produced information that could not have been known to her by normal means, this did not necessarily mean that she was getting the information from the world of the spirits. Perhaps she was really reading the mind of some living person, or looking into the contents of a locked box or closed book by clairvoyance. Perhaps this information was not coming through the spirits at all, but through extrasensory perception or ESP.

Now ESP is a long way from being proven in the minds of most scientists, but it seems infinitely more reasonable than spirit communication. Besides, it's a lot easier to investigate. The researcher does not have to deal exclusively with mediums, who are traditionally tempermental, unreliable, and all too often just plain crooked. The bulk of psychical research and parapsychology for the last half century has been concentrated on examining the claims for extrasensory perception.

What about the problem of survival, with which psychical research really started? Dr. J. B. Rhine, formerly of Duke University, and the grand old man of American parapsychology, sadly concluded that there has never really been a successful scientific confirmation of the survival hypothesis. It was a hard admission for Rhine to make, for he had first become interested in the subject through spiritualism. While some parapsychologists would disagree with his conclusion, most responsible ones would not. Most of the claims of "absolute proof" of survival after death, or "true" experience in communicating with the dead, are made by individuals who have not worked professionally in the field—though parapsychologists are certainly more sympathetic to the survival hypothesis than scientists in most other fields.

While there have been no really successful scientific investigations of the possibility of life after death, the scientific study

Dr. Ian Stevenson

of reincarnation can hardly be said to have begun at all. In a listing of recommended books on mediumship and survival, put out by the American Society for Psychical Research, there is only one book listed under the heading of Reincarnation. It is *Twenty Cases Suggestive of Reincarnation* by Dr. Ian Stevenson. Dr. Stevenson is not only the leading scientific student of reincarnation in the West, he is practically the only one.

Dr. Stevenson was born in Montreal, Canada, on October 31, 1918. He received his medical training at McGill University, and went on to specialize in psychiatry. In 1957 he became chairman of the Department of Neurology and Psychiatry at the University of Virginia, a post that he held for ten years. Since that time he has been Alumni Professor of Psychiatry at Virginia.

The University of Virginia is one of a handful of American universities that has some tradition in the study of parapsychology. Dr. Stevenson, who has long been interested in parapsychology, particularly the problems of survival, has found the atmosphere congenial for his work.

Dr. Stevenson has attempted to approach the problem of reincarnation from two angles, by collecting case histories, and by trying to set up an experiment in reincarnation. Of the two, the case history approach is the better known. What Dr. Stevenson and his associates have done is collect accounts from around the world which seem to indicate reincarnation, and then investigate the authenticity of these accounts as closely as possible. It is very much the sort of approach used by other psychical researchers in investigating tales of ghosts or poltergeists. To date, Dr. Stevenson has nearly 1,000 cases in his files. Naturally the cases are of widely varying evidential value but the best of them are included in his book of twenty cases.

Most of these cases concern children who appear to remember a former life. The cases are spontaneous, that is, they do not involve hypnotized subjects or individuals who were in any other way induced to recall past lives. There are no Bridey Murphys in Dr. Stevenson's collection.

One of the best, if not *the* best single case, concerns a boy from

Lebanon named Imad Elawar. His family belonged to the religious sect known as the Druses, which believes in the transmigration of souls and thus is likely to take stories about reincarnation quite seriously.

What makes the Imad Elawar case most impressive, however, is that Dr. Stevenson just happened to be on the scene to watch it develop. In mid-March, 1964, he visited the Lebanese village of Kornayel, fifteen miles east of the capital city of Beirut. It was his intention to investigate an entirely different case and he heard of Imad by accident.

In 1964, Imad was five years old. Since the age of two he had apparently been making references to a previous life by mentioning the names of people or describing events that had nothing to do with his present life.

Imad's story was particularly suitable for investigation because he claimed that his previous life had been in the town of Khriby, a mere fifteen miles away from his present home. In addition, he was not claiming to have lived in Khriby in the distant and misty past, but only a few years before his current birth. It was the sort of case that could be investigated.

Though the villages of Kornayel and Khriby were close, the only connecting road ran over twenty-five twisting miles through the mountains. Contacts between the two villages were infrequent, and Dr. Stevenson felt that it was unlikely that Imad would have known anybody in the other village. Yet Imad insisted that his former family name was Bouhamzy, and that he had lived in Khriby.

Imad's parents, though believers in reincarnation, had first tended to disregard their young son's stories of a previous life. Then one day when Imad was four he was being taken for a walk by his grandmother. He suddenly rushed up to a stranger on the street and hugged him. The puzzled stranger asked, "Do you know me?" and Imad replied, "Yes, you were my neighbor." The stranger was a visitor from the village of Khriby and had lived near the house of a man named Bouhamzy.

After that the boy's parents began to treat his claims more seriously. Somewhat later Imad's father went to Khriby, for the first time in his life, in order to attend a funeral. He inquired about members of the Bouhamzy family, and some of them were pointed out to him, though he made no attempt to speak to them.

When Dr. Stevenson arrived in Kornayel, Imad's parents had fully accepted his story, and had even begun to make some assumptions about it that proved unjustified. Wrote Dr. Stevenson, "His parents passed on to me some of the inferences which they themselves had made in their effort to find some coherent patterns in the whole story. . . As it turned out, however, the errors of inference made by Imad's family add considerably to the evidence of their honesty and also to the improbability that they themselves could have provided a source or channel for the information given by Imad."

Among the first words that Imad had ever spoken were the names "Jamile" and "Mahmoud." He made many references to Jamile's beauty and charm. He spoke of a "sister" named Huda, and a whole crowd of friends, and/or relatives. He specifically referred to a friend whose name he gave as Yousef el Galibi. He also spoke of an accident in which a man's legs had been crushed, and the injuries subsequently led to his death. Imad often appeared elated that he himself could walk. None of these names or incidents had anything to do with Imad Elawar's present life.

His parents concluded that the boy, in a previous life, had been Mahmoud Bouhamzy of Khriby, that he had a wife named

Jamile, and that he had been fatally injured in a truck accident.

When Dr. Stevenson heard of this tale he was eager to check it out. So, accompanied by Imad and his father, the doctor drove to Khriby, the village of Imad's supposed previous incarnation.

The initial results of the investigation were discouraging. There was a man named Mahmoud Bouhamzy in Khriby, but he was very much alive. There was another Bouhamzy, named Said, who had been killed in the sort of truck accident that Imad had described. But Said Bouhamzy had no connection with a woman named Jamile, nor did many of the other details of Said Bouhamzy's life fit with Imad's recollections. To make matters even more confusing, there already was a child who claimed to be the reincarnation of Said Bouhamzy, and this identification had been accepted by Said's family.

Just as this promising case appeared to be falling to pieces, Dr. Stevenson was told of a third Bouhamzy, a cousin of the fatally injured Said. This man's name was Ibrahim, and he had lived with a woman named Jamile, though they had never married. Ibrahim Bouhamzy contracted tuberculosis and died in 1949 at the age of twenty-five. He spent the last year of his life in a sanitarium. The disease had affected his spine, and for two months before his death he had been unable to walk.

Dr. Stevenson took Imad through the house in which Ibrahim Bouhamzy had lived. He counted sixteen correct statements or identifications that Imad made about the house in which he had never been before, at least in his present lifetime. In Dr. Stevenson's view he correctly located two sheds, the place where the goats were kept, a place for storage of tools, and a number of other places that he should not have known.

Dr. Stevenson believed that much of his initial confusion over identification had come from the fact that he had accepted many of the parent's interpretations, rather than listening more closely to the boy's own direct statements. Imad never said that he had been killed in a truck accident; he talked about the accident. Ibrahim had been Said's cousin and the two had also been close friends. Ibrahim may well have been a witness to the truck accident which took place in 1943. According to Ibrahim's friends, he had been deeply affected by his cousin's death, and had always blamed the truck driver.

Ibrahim's own incapacity before his death may have led to Imad's surprise and pleasure at being able to walk in this life.

Again, Imad never said he had been married to the woman called Jamile. Imad's parents simply made that assumption because he talked about her so often.

Ibrahim Bouhamzy had been a quarrelsome and occasionally violent fellow during his lifetime. He once shot someone during a fight. Imad's father said that his boy also had a reputation for belligerence, and had a tendency to brood over insults, real and imagined. One odd fact was that in school Imad was an exceptionally good student of French, though no one in his family knew the language. Ibrahim Bouhamzy, however, had once served in the French army and spoke the language fluently.

One of the complicating factors that Dr. Stevenson ran across in this case was Sleimann Bouhamzy, who was twenty-one years old when Dr. Stevenson interviewed him in 1964. This young man claimed to be the reincarnation of Said Bouhamzy, the man killed in the truck accident. The death had occurred on June 8, 1943. On December 3, 1943, Said's only sister gave birth to Sleimann. This made Sleimann the reincarnation of his own uncle.

Dr. Stevenson found this case unusual because Sleimann had been conceived, though not yet born, at the time of Said's death.

Dr. Stevenson, however, has recorded a number of other cases where a child claimed to be a person who had died after the child was conceived or actually born.

When Sleimann was interviewed by Dr. Stevenson in 1964 he claimed to have fogotten most of the memories of his previous life. But the details of his death caused by the truck accident were still vivid. He had an intense fear of any sort of motor vehicle, and when he was small would not even approach an automobile. He also had a fear of bandages and blood, and once fainted when he saw someone's head swathed in bandages.

As a small child Sleimann was supposed to have called his mother "sister" and adopted a paternal attitude toward Said's sons, although they were older than he. He claimed to be able to recognize all of Said's old friends and family members. Said's family had come to fully accept the identification and, according to Dr. Stevenson's report, were planning to support Sleimann's further education.

Of the two cases the one of Said/Sleimann is more intriguing, because of the idea of someone being reborn as his own nephew. But the quality of the evidence is much less satisfactory. Though Sleimann was not a resident of Khriby, Said's village, he did visit it frequently. As a relative of Said, he may well have heard of his death in the accident. This could easily have made a deep impression on his young mind, an impression that he was not necessarily conscious of. This, rather than reincarnation, could explain the boy's fear of motor cars, bandages, and blood.

The case of Ibrahim/Imad is not so easy to explain away. Dr. Stevenson had naturally considered the possibility that the entire case was a hoax. But this seemed highly unlikely, since he had come upon it entirely by accident. Imad's family had no way of knowing that a Western professor was coming to their village to study reincarnation, thus no particular motive for cooking up a story beforehand. Dr. Stevenson also felt that the very errors in the story told by the boy's parents tended to indicate that no fakery was involved.

However, while the fact that the boy's parents gave Dr. Stevenson many wrong details at first may tend to indicate that they were not handing out a carefully prepared false story, it also muddies up the evidence. The parents thought the boy was the incarnation of Mahmoud Bouhamzy. When Dr. Stevenson found this was impossible, he re-examined, and reinterpreted, the evidence. But how much of this interpretation was influenced by the researcher's desire to find evidence to support his reincarnation hypothesis?

Here we must say a word about the subject of scientific objectivity. There is a general, but incorrect, impression that all scientists approach an experiment or a study with "total objectivity," that is, that they have no opinions on the subject they are studying, and no particular feeling about which way the study turns out. This is, of course, impossible. Scientists, like the rest of us, have opinions. Scientists rarely go into a project without having a pretty good idea about how they think it will come out, and usually a strong desire to see it come out in a particular way. There is nothing "unscientific" or "dishonest" about this, presuming that the scientist reports the facts he has gathered as accurately as possible. In many areas of science there is a great deal of fierce controversy over how the results of a particular experiment or a particular finding should be interpreted.

Dr. Stevenson reported the negative, as well as the positive, in this case. He said that the boy was not very good at identifying buildings in the town in which he was supposed to have lived.

Once, while apparently pointing in the direction of the house in which Ibrahim Bouhamzy had lived, he also called attention to another nearby house which had nothing to do with Ibrahim Bouhamzy. He did not recognize the houses in Ibrahim's immediate neighborhood. The people of the village said, however, that it had changed a good deal in the past few years.

Dr. Stevenson himself was more impressed by the fact that Imad appeared to be able to recognize the inside of Ibrahim's house than his failure to recognize the neighborhood. So the evidence points both ways. One can explain away both his failures and his successes.

This case, possibly the best and most carefully recorded on record, is a long way from providing the sort of conclusive evidence necessary for science to take the subject of reincarnation more seriously. Dr. Stevenson himself provides three "serious contenders" to explain the facts. First, ESP—that is, that the boy was somehow getting this information from the mind of another living person, presumably one of Ibrahim's relatives or friends. Second, possession by a spirit, probably that of the dead Ibrahim. Third—and the explanation that he clearly favors—reincarnation.

There is, however, another and more prosaic explanation—wishful thinking. It would be a combination of parents who believed in reincarnation, as Imad's parents did, and a researcher who was sympathetic toward such an explanation coming together and interpreting a string of childish statements as proof of their beliefs.

While none of Dr. Stevenson's other nineteen "suggestive" cases is up to the level of the Ibrahim/Imad case in quality evidence, there are others which indicate a different and possibly significant attitude toward reincarnation.

The Tlingit Indians of southeastern Alaska not only believe in reincarnation, they believe that a person is generally reincarnated within his own family and possesses a measure of control over his next incarnation.

Increasing contact with outsiders, however, has weakened the old Tlingit belief. William George (a pseudonym chosen by Dr. Stevenson), a fisherman of the Tlingit tribe, had believed in reincarnation for most of his life. But as he grew older he began to entertain some doubts about the doctrine and he began to yearn for a concrete form of proof. Several times he told his son Reginald and daughter-in-law Susan, "If there is anything to this rebirth business I will come back and be your son."

In mid-1949 when William George was about sixty, he handed his favorite gold watch to his son and said, "I'll come back. Keep this watch for me. I am going to be your son. If there is anything like that [reincarnation] I'll do it."

A few weeks later the old man's fishing boat was lost at sea. His body was never recovered.

At about that time Susan George became pregnant with the ninth of her ten children. Nine months later, while she was in labor, she had a vivid dream that her dead father-in-law spoke to her and said that he was waiting to see his son.

Mrs. George had awakened from the anesthetic confused and half-expecting to see the dead man's ghost standing by her bedside. Instead, she saw her new baby boy. But the baby had distinct birthmarks on his left shoulder and left forearm. These were in the same spots which his grandfather had shown prominent birthmarks. The parents gave the child the name William George, Jr. This was in accord with long-standing Tlingit tradition.

The watch that William George, Sr. had intended as a test of reincarnation was put away in a jewelry box. When William George, Jr. was between four and five years old his mother was going through her jewlery box. All the contents were spread out in the bedroom. The boy came into the room, noticed the watch, and said: "That's my watch." It was only with great difficulty that his mother persuaded him that she should be allowed to keep it safely for him. For some years the boy continued to talk about "my watch." When Dr. Stevenson visited the family the watch was taken out and given to the boy, who handled it fondly.

There were a few other points that Dr. Stevenson noted about this case. William George, Sr. had injured his left foot, and walked with a pronounced limp. The boy also walked with a limp, though a far less severe one.

At one point the boy, when he was about four, mentioned that his "sister" had just passed by. Actually the woman who had passed by was his great aunt, his grandfather's sister. This might have been nothing more than a childish slip of the tongue, but it was very impressive to his parents.

Reginald George also claimed that the child appeared to have an excellent, almost uncanny, knowledge of the best places to fish. William, Sr. had been a superb fisherman, highly respected among his fellow tribesman as a man who always knew the best places to fish.

Intriguing as this case is, it has some serious shortcomings as evidence. Dr. Stevenson had to rely almost entirely upon the memories of parents, who themselves believed strongly in reincarnation. When Dr. Stevenson interviewed William George, Jr. the boy seemed to have forgotten most memories he once might have had about a past life. He could only recall his special feeling toward his grandfather's watch.

Back in 1840, when Alaska was still owned by Russia, a

Russian scholar reported on the religion of the Tlingits to the Imperial Academy of Sciences in St. Petersburg. He noted that the Tlingits "believe that dead persons return to this world, but only among their relatives." He also remarked, "For this reason, if a pregnant woman sees, often in her dreams, a deceased relative, she believes that this man has entered into her; or perhaps if they discover on the body of a newborn some resemblance with a deceased person such as a birthmark or defect which they knew had existed in the body of the deceased person, they begin to believe firmly that this same person has returned to earth, and for the same reason they give the newborn baby the name of the deceased person."

The case of William George, Senior and Junior, fits that description neatly—almost too neatly. The family had already been alerted by William, Senior, that he was going to try and come back as their son. When the old man did disappear, the parents were surely at least half-expecting their unborn child to be the old man's reincarnation. Since they held the old man in great esteem they must have wished that he would return as their son. When the baby turned out to be a boy they would have watched him closely for any sign that he was indeed his grandfather reincarnated. Small and perhaps meaningless incidents could have been blown entirely out of proportion.

Even the apparent recognition of William, Senior's, gold watch may in fact, have had no special meaning at all. The child could have overheard the parents discussing the watch and William, Senior's, desire to use it as a test of reincarnation. This would have planted in the child's head the idea that the watch was his. Perhaps he just took a fancy to a pretty object, and declared that it was his because he liked it. Children often do that sort of thing under circumstances which have nothing whatever to do with reincarnation. The parents, however, would have interpreted this simple childish act as something much more portentous, because of their previous belief in reincarnation.

One of the major criticisms of Dr. Stevenson's collection of cases is that the vast majority of them are drawn from among people like the Tlingits, or the Druses of Lebanon, or the people of India (a large percentage of his cases come from India). These are people who already believe in reincarnation.

Professor C. T. K. Chari, Madras, India, reviewed some of Dr. Stevenson's cases in the *International Journal of Parapsychology*. He stressed that one had to keep in mind the possibility that "India's notoriously 'pro' attitude toward reincarnationist beliefs may unconsciously and systematically influence the testimony of parents and interested bystanders."

Dr. Stevenson, somewhat put off by what he regards as an overcautious view even on the part of parapsychologists toward reincarnation, warned his colleagues against losing "the adventurousness which every field requires to advance." But parapsychologists are among the most adventurous of all scientists. If many of them feel unsure and uneasy with the evidence collected for reincarnation, then it is safe to assume that scientists in other fields are even less impressed.

A basic problem is that the sort of spontaneous case histories recorded in *Twenty Cases Suggestive of Reincarnation* are never going to provide the kind of solid, unambiguous information required as scientific proof. To get that sort of data some type of controlled experiment is necessary.

For years psychical researchers have been trying to devise a standard test for survival after death. Early pioneers of psychical research left sealed messages that they were to try to communicate back to the living, through a medium, after their own death. But there are severe problems with such message tests. If living persons knew the contents of the message, this opened the possibility that the medium learned the contents of the message through fraud, or picked it up by ESP from the mind of the living person, (assuming, of course, that one accepts ESP as a proven reality, and most psychical researchers do).

If, however, one left behind a sealed message that no one knew, that would be a test that could be used only once. In order to check the accuracy of a mediumistic communication the message would have to be unsealed. If the message were wrong, the test would be rendered useless anyway. Then, for those who believe in the reality of ESP, there is still the problem of clairvoyance, seeing distant objects or events. Would it not be possible for the medium to look inside the sealed envelope? Thus, one would never really know if a correct message could be taken as evidence for survival after death.

All manner of variations of this type of test have been devised. One of the most ingenious was conceived by Dr. Stevenson. The test uses an ordinary combination lock. He suggests that an individual can take a lock, set the combination himself—a combination of such a lock is usually a series of six numerals or letters. The owner of the lock then memorizes the combination, and tries to transmit it back through a medium after his death. The advantage, of course, is that the test can be reused many times, until some medium comes up with the correct combination. The odds against getting the correct combination by pure chance are astronomical.

Objections can also be raised. The obvious one is that the person setting the combination might tell someone else what it is, even if he wasn't supposed to. This would destroy the secrecy necessary for the experiment. Others argue that a medium might, in some extrasensory manner, become aware of the combination before the person's death, or alternately in some manner get a clairvoyant peek at the workings of the lock, and thus learn the combination without the aid of a message from the beyond.

Still, even with these objections, the lock test does represent an improvement over the old sealed letters. Dr. Stevenson himself has several set locks, and will bring them to the attention of a medium after the death of the owners. No significant results have as yet been reported.

This gives you a glimpse at the problems involved in attempting a controlled test of the theory of survival of the personality after death. In the survival theory it is assumed that the spirit is in some way or another near the place where the individual experienced bodily death, and that if contact is possible, it could occur within a reasonably short time after death. In addition, most tests of survival also assume the validity of mediumistic communication with the dead.

But in reincarnation the problems are infinitely more difficult. If one accepts the theory of reincarnation at all, one assumes that an individual can be reincarnated a hundred or a thousand years after death, and that he or she might return at some distant place.

Dr. Stevenson is currently conducting a broad project that he calls planned evidence of survival after death. A major part of this project concerns reincarnation, and is based upon the belief or theory or possibly hope that we have some control over our next incarnation.

Though the project isn't really secret, Dr. Stevenson actively tries to discourage publicity about it. His reasons are simple; interest in survival in general and reincarnation in particular is so high that any publicity results in a flood of mail that Dr. Stevenson has neither the time nor staff to answer. He is also wary, as are many parapyschologists, that a lot of publicity will tend to sensationalize his work, and make him look bad in the eyes of his scientific colleagues. Parapsychologists who have often been scorned by other scientists are very sensitive about their respectability.

However, since the project has already received considerable publicity, there seems no harm in describing it in a general way.

Subjects are given a twelve-page form in which they are asked to supply general information about themselves, including a photograph and a fingerprint. The subjects are then asked to write down any thoughts or feelings they may have about their own previous lives. The questionnaire places particular stress on any traits, physical or behavioral, that a subject feels may have been carried over from past lives or may be carried into future ones.

The questionnaire then turns to an exploration of the subjects' desires and expectations concerning their next incarnation. Where would the subject like to be reborn, who would he like to be associated with in his next incarnation, how long a period would he like to have between lives, and so on.

The final section of the form is to be detached and given to a relative or friend who will fill it out after the subject's death, and then send it to Dr. Stevenson. This section concerns such things as the manner of the subject's death and any last words or other noteworthy features of the subject's last hours or minutes.

Interest in this project has been so great that Dr. Stevenson has been forced to limit sending the form to persons sixty-five years of age or older. The obvious reason for this, says Dr.

Stevenson, is that such persons "are more likely to die and therefore contribute to the success of the experiment in the fairly near future than are younger persons." Moreover, persons are required to state in writing that they will fill out the form and return it promptly. He is not interested in idle curiosity seekers.

What results have been obtained in the four years since this project was first begun? Dr. Stevenson flatly refuses to give out any information but, again, not because he is being deliberately secretive or trying to make mysteries. "In accordance with the policy adopted by scientists, I do not have any statement I wish to make about this form for use in a popular article or book until I have prepared a report for scientific colleagues," he said. Not all scientists follow such a policy, but many do, and as I mentioned, parapsychologists are very sensitive about the subject of scientific respectability. So far, no scientific report has been published, and the project clearly is a long-term one.

However, a few conclusions are obvious. First, this planned evidence of survival project does not seem designed to produce the really hard evidence that would be necessary for broad acceptance of the idea of reincarnation in the West. At best it will give parapsychologists a body of information concerning an individual's personal beliefs about reincarnation, and it may give them a place to look for evidence in the future.

If an individual says that he expects to be reborn in a particular place and a particular time, then researchers might be on hand to see what happens. If, for example, the Tlingit Indian, George Wilson, Sr. had filled out one of Dr. Stevenson's forms before his death, then researchers could have followed the early life of George Wilson, Jr. more carefully. They could have witnessed the reaction when the boy was first shown the gold watch, and they could have questioned him about memories of a previous life before they began to slip away. Using the form, the researchers would have been able to establish a better case then was possible by relying on chance and spontaneous recall.

Whether the forms now piling up in Dr. Stevenson's files will someday provide a significant body of evidence supporting the theory of reincarnation, only time will tell. But clearly, from the embarrassingly large response Dr. Stevenson has had to news of his project, the subject is of compelling interest to many, many Americans.

A Selected Bibliography

Though a huge number of books have been written on the subject of reincarnation, an embarrassingly small number are of any value at all to the general reader. A considerable percentage of available books are explorations of Eastern mysticism or esoteric occultism, which are virtually meaningless to the uninitiated. There is also a fair amount of trash cranked out for a sensation-hungry public.

The books listed below do not by any means represent a complete cross section of available books on reincarnation. I have stayed almost entirely away from books on reincarnation in Eastern religion, because the subject is not discussed in this volume. There are only a few genuinely occult works on the list, and I have tried to include only the best written and most influential of the trash.

Bernstein, Morey. *The Search for Bridey Murphy*. New York: Doubleday, 1965.

This revised edition of the original Bridey Murphy book published in 1956 contains much additional material.

Blavatsky, Helena P. *The Secret Doctrine*. Adyar, India: Theosophical Publishing Company, 1938.

H.P.B.'s best known and longest work.

Boswell, Harriet A. *Master Guide to Psychism*. West Nyack, New York: Parker, 1969.

An attempt to place reincarnation within a whole field of psychic phenomena.

Cayce, Edgar Evans. *Edgar Cayce on Atlantis.* New York: Paperback Library, 1968.

Cayce, Hugh Lynn. *Venture Inward.* New York: Harper, 1964.

The Cayce children, particularly Hugh Lynn, have written or edited what threatens to become an endless series of books on their late father's life and work. These are two of the books which deal heavily with reincarnation.

Cerminara, Gina. *Many Mansions.* New York: Sloane, 1950.

An early and extremely popular book about Cayce's ideas of Karma and reincarnation.

Cohen, Daniel. *Masters of the Occult.* New York: Dodd, Mead, 1971.

Contains biographical sketches of Helena P. Blavatsky and L. Ron Hubbard.

De Camp, L. Sprague, and De Camp, Catherine. *Spirits, Stars and Spells.* New York: Canaveral Press, 1966.

A witty and highly skeptical account of a whole range of occult and magical subjects.

Ebon, Martin, ed. *The Psychic Scene.* New York: Signet, 1974.

———. *Reincarnation in the Twentieth Century.* New York: Signet, 1970.

Ebon has edited a series on everything from ESP to Witchcraft. His intelligent introduction is usually the best part of each book.

Evans, Christopher. *Cults of Unreason.* New York: Farrar, Straus & Giroux, 1973.

A British psychologist looks at modern cults, particularly Scientology.

Flournoy, Theodore. *From India to the Planet Mars.* New York: University Books, 1963.

The classic study of the incarnating medium, Hélène Smith.

Gardner, Martin. *Fads and Fallacies in the Name of Science.* New York: Dover, 1957.

Many of the fads of the 1940s and 1950s, including Bridey Murphy get a good going over in this book.

Grant, Joan. *Far Memory.* New York: Harper, 1965.

———. *Winged Pharaoh.* New York: Harper, 1938.
The author's most famous book about her past lives, and an explanation of how she is supposed to remember what all the rest of us forget.

Hamel, Frank. *Human Animals.* New York: University Press, 1969.
Miss Hamel (yes, Miss) has collected a really dandy batch of stories of transmigration, magical transformations, and the like.

Head, Joseph, and Cranston, S. L. *Reincarnation—an East-West Anthology.* Wheaton, Illinois: Theosophical Publishing House, 1961.
A fine collection of quotes and other short pieces on reincarnation and immortality.

Holzer, Hans. *Born Again: The Truth about Reincarnation.* New York: Doubleday, 1970.
A typical collection of unproven reincarnation tales.

Kelsey, Denys, and Grant, Joan. *Many Lifetimes.* New York: Doubleday, 1967.
The far memory adept and her psychiatrist husband write about reincarnation.

Langley, Noel. *Edgar Cayce on Reincarnation.* New York: Warner, 1967.
Hugh Lynn Cayce wrote the foreword for this book. It is another in the series on America's most popular psychic.

Malko, George. *Scientology: The Now Religion.* New York: Delacorte, 1970.
A critical examination of L. Ron Hubbard's religion. Scientologists hated it.

Montgomery, Ruth. *Here and Hereafter.* New York: Coward-McCann, 1968.
The past lives of many supposedly famous but often unnamed people. Popular and pleasant to read, but of no evidential value.

Moore, Marcia, and Douglas, Mark. *Reincarnation, Key to Immortality.* York Cliffs, Maine: Arcane Publishers, 1968.
A bit diffuse, but not a bad introduction to the subject for believers.

Ostrander, Sheila and Schroeder, Lynn. *Psychic Discoveries Behind the Iron Curtain.* Englewood Cliffs, New Jersey: Prentice-Hall, 1970.

Contains a chapter on the supposed Russian work with "artificial reincarnation." The authors exaggerate.

Rawcliffe, D. H. *Occult and Supernatural Phenomena.* New York: Dover, 1959.

A skeptical psychologist looks at a broad range of phenomena.

Roberts, Jane. *The Seth Material.* Englewood Cliffs, New Jersey: Prentice-Hall, 1970.

Lectures on reincarnation and other subjects delivered through medium Roberts, from the spirit of Seth.

Smith, Susy. *ESP and Hypnosis.* New York: Macmillan, 1973.

———. *Reincarnation for the Millions.* Los Angeles: Sherbourn Press, 1967.

Popular books on psychic subjects, but better than most.

Somerlott, Robert. "*Here, Mr. Splitfoot.*" New York: Viking, 1971.

The subtitle reads, "An Informal Exploration into Modern Occultism."

Spence, Lewis. *An Encyclopedia of Occultism.* New York: University Books, 1960.

A huge collection of brief articles on reincarnation and lots of other things.

Stearn, Jess. *Edgar Cayce, the Sleeping Prophet.* New York: Doubleday, 1967.

———. *A Prophet in His Own Country: The Story of the Young Edgar Cayce.* New York: Morrow, 1974.

———. *The Search for a Soul, Taylor Caldwell's Psychic Lives.* New York: Doubleday, 1973.

———. *The Search for the Girl with the Blue Eyes.* New York: Doubleday, 1968.

Though Stearn's books are extremely popular, it is difficult to separate fact from imagination.

Steiger, Brad. *The Enigma of Reincarnation.* New York: Ace, 1967.
Fairly standard popular occult fare.

Stevenson, Ian. *Twenty Cases Suggestive of Reincarnation.* New York: American Society for Psychical Research, 1966.
The only reincarnation book around with any claim to scientific accuracy.

Sugrue, Thomas. *There Is a River.* New York: Holt, 1942.
The best of the many Edgar Cayce biographies.

Williams, Gertrude M. *Madame Blavatsky, Priestess of the Occult.* New York: Knopf, 1946.
A first-rate biography of this marvelous character.

Index

INDEX

INDEX

The Author

DANIEL COHEN is a free-lance writer and former managing editor of *Science Digest* magazine. He has written numerous books for adults and young readers on subjects ranging from science to the supernatural. His previous books include *In Search of Ghosts* and *The Magic Art of Foreseeing the Future*. He also appears frequently on radio and television and has lectured at colleges and universities throughout the country.

Mr. Cohen is a native of Chicago and holds a degree in journalism from the University of Illinois. He lives with his wife, who is also a writer, their daughter, and a collection of cats and dogs in Port Jervis, New York.